Y0-BJN-143

3 9082 03273503 0

J 791.53
P

PHILPOTT, Alexis Robert

Eight plays for hand puppets, by members
of the Educational Puppetry Assn., ed., by
A. R. Philpott. Plays,
inc. [1968] 74p. Orig. pub. in Britain
by J. Garnet Miller, inc. bds., 4.00

*1. Puppets and puppet plays. Educational
Puppetry Association, London.*

COPY 84

5 and up

Trenton Public Library
2790 Westfield Road
Trenton, Mich. 48183

69877 N72

MAR 3 1973

EIGHT PLAYS FOR HAND PUPPETS

NOTE

No fees are required for non-professional performances. The Educational Puppetry Association would appreciate receiving a programme or a report of any public performance.

Professional puppeteers wishing to produce any of the plays should get in touch with the Hon. Secretary of the Association, at 23a, Southampton Place, London, W.C.1 before going into production.

EIGHT PLAYS FOR HAND PUPPETS

by members of
The Educational Puppetry Association

edited by
A. R. PHILPOTT

Trenton Public Library
2790 Westfield Road
Trenton, Mich. 48183

J. GARNET MILLER LTD.
13 Tottenham Street
LONDON, W.1

FIRST PUBLISHED BY
J. GARNET MILLER LTD
IN 1968

Printed in Great Britain by
GILMOUR & DEAN LTD., HAMILTON & LONDON

© 1968
THE EDUCATIONAL PUPPETRY ASSOCIATION

CONTENTS

page

INTRODUCTION — vii

PUPPET PLAY PRODUCTION — xi

THE AUDIENCE — xvi

THE PLAYS

PUNCH AND THE HEARTLESS GIANT
by Luke Gertler — 1

OWL'S BIRTHDAY
by Pantopuck the Puppetman — 16

THE SILVER KEY
by Children of a Junior-mixed School — 23

PEPI AND SOMBRERO by Joyce Thomson — 38

A CANADIAN FAIRY TALE
adapted by Edna Rist — 46

THE GINGERBREAD BOY
by a Primary School child — 51

THE EGG by Violet M. Philpott — 57

THE LONELY GIANT
by the London Group of the E.P.A. — 65

ACKNOWLEDGMENTS

The Educational Puppetry Association thanks all who have helped in the preparation of this book: the authors who contributed the plays; Miss A. D. Smith, Head Teacher of the Eliot Bank Primary School, for permission to include *The Gingerbread Boy*, and Miss G. G. Baldry, Head Teacher of Holbeach Junior Mixed School, for *The Silver Key;* the members of the Book Committee who made the selection from the many plays submitted; and Mr. and Mrs. A. S. Burack of PLAYS, INC., Boston, U.S.A. for many valuable suggestions regarding the text.

INTRODUCTION

In searching for material for puppet play production there are two approaches open to us: we can use published plays or we can make scripts from existing or original themes. In either case we must first understand the dramatic scope of the puppet, its possibilities, its limits. This is equally true for beginners or professional puppeteers.

An experienced producer of puppet plays will see at once the puppet qualities of the selection of plays here offered. A beginner, or one with a little experience, in the course of producing these plays will gain that essential understanding of what is good material for puppets, of what is perhaps even better on the puppet stage than on the human stage.

These plays have all been produced with considerable success with hand (or "glove") puppets. They may be used as frameworks on which your own puppets can build. They may be freely adapted to circumstances—age group of performers, type of stage being used.

Some of the plays are essentially for group work (e.g. *The Lonely Giant*, with its live giant); and others have been presented as solo items (e.g. *The Egg*, and *The Heartless Giant*) but may equally well be produced with one performer for each character.

PLAY SOURCES

Plays for puppets come into being in several ways. There may be an idea for a plot first, with a group of related characters, or the puppets may be made first, perhaps independently by several makers, and through spontaneous interaction when these characters meet on stage a play begins to evolve. The idea for the

EIGHT PLAYS FOR HAND PUPPETS

Lonely Giant came from one member of a group and developed into its final form through discussion following the trying out of variations of each phase of the action and dialogue, with the producer studying results from the audience point of view. The starting point for the *Silver Key* was a four-line verse and a list of possible characters.

There are ready-made themes to be found in abundance in traditional folk tales (an item based on a Canadian tale has been included), fables, fairy tales, animal stories, legends and ballads—but these must not only be given dramatic form, they must be suitable for production *with puppets*.

The titles of some stories immediately stir the imagination: *The Magic Sack*, *The Wonderful Glove*, *The Lucky Fisherman*. Such words as *magic*, *wonderful*, *lucky* (*wise*, *silly*, *enchanted*, *lonely*, etc.) make a powerful impact on mind and feelings. A title on a programme or a spoken announcement of a play with such a word in it creates expectancy in the audience. This expectancy must be fulfilled during the performance.

THE AUDIENCE

When people go to see a puppet play, their interest is centred in what happens on the stage and how the puppets act. What the puppets *do* is more important than what they say, although of course what they say must be related to the action. The play may be witty, but it will be successful only if the speech follows naturally from the action of the unfolding story.

It cannot be too strongly emphasized that a play for hand puppets should *not* be learned word for word: it should remain flexible, and this will ensure spontaneity at every performance.

INTRODUCTION

Dialect and colloquial speech forms can be introduced in place of the scripted dialogue if the producer feels this will be appropriate and if the performers have the necessary flair to do this effectively. In *Pepi and Sombrero*, for instance, the Mexican flavour of this item can be created by the use of "Si, si, senor" and similar phrases. If a Mexican "accent" is introduced because the performers have identified with the Mexican characters, this will be fine; otherwise a few Spanish phrases will be sufficient.

DIALOGUE AND ACTION

Because action has priority over speech, the dialogue needs to be economical; puppets can rarely make long speeches effectively. The speech must be audible, as inaudibility will ruin the best of plots. It is one of the functions of the producer to ensure this audibility. Puppetry is not primarily a vehicle for speech training, but both speech and vocabulary can be improved through the medium of the play performed, quite incidentally and painlessly.

The device of having a Narrator linking different parts of a play should only be used if this adds something positive to the performance. If having a Narrator is merely an easy answer to technical problems, then probably a wrong choice of play has been made, as the audience comes primarily *to watch*, not simply to listen.

The action of a play should consist of a logical sequence of events. Anything which does not forward the plot should be pruned out. The temptation to add "frills" to cover up places which seem "a little thin" in the play should be resisted. Instead, the question should be put: *Why* is it thin? Discover at what point interest begins to diminish and what was happening

ix

EIGHT PLAYS FOR HAND PUPPETS

at that point. Look for the logical consequence of that happening. This examination of the play may well cause it to take a new and more exciting direction.

It is essential to be critical at all times; anything irrelevant or artificial should be ruthlessly discarded. It is not important if the finished play bears little relation to the original idea. What *is* important is that the final creation is enjoyed both by performers and audience alike.

Finally, those who have made this book of plays possible hope it will widen the horizon as to puppet play possibilities and lead on to successful original work.

PUPPET PLAY PRODUCTION

The producer of puppet plays needs a clear understanding of his medium and must know just what
puppets can and cannot do. For instance, the hand
puppet ("glove" type), having no legs, cannot kick a
ball; but it can certainly throw and catch. This type is
also not likely to make a very successful attempt at
riding a bicycle, but, in puppet fashion, can drive
around in a car.

Before attempting complete plays, beginners should
first become at home in the puppet stage, discovering
the maximum range of action for each puppet, how to
make exits and entries effectively, how to handle stage
properties securely, how to avoid awkward and un-
comfortable positions. A character entering from
"stage left" and on the performer's *left* hand will
usually be able to face a character on the right more
easily than if on the performer's right hand. The best
choice of hand for a character entering "stage centre"
will depend on the next moves to be made. The producer will check such points. The actual production
of some of the plays in this book will result in a good
working knowledge of puppet action.

The Puppet Stage

It is essential to have a stage of the design and di-
mensions to give maximum freedom of movement both
to performers and to puppets. If performers have to
work in cramped conditions then the range of action
of the puppets will be severely restricted. The acting
area of an *open type* stage permits greater variety of
action and is to be preferred to the traditional Punch-

EIGHT PLAYS FOR HAND PUPPETS

and-Judy type of booth with its proscenium and side curtains. The open type stage also gives better viewing for the spectators. It has a rigid *backscreen* in place of the old style backdrop. The backscreen is made of fibreboard or plywood; two or three exits can be cut in this, greatly increasing the dramatic possibilities. Puppets can pop in and out in a variety of ways, peep in and disappear, chase each other back and forth. Actual doors can be fitted (hinged) or the exits can be curtained.

Scenery can be attached to the backscreen, such as the front of a house or palace, barn, giant's cave. Instructions for making this type of stage can be found in *The Puppet Book*, edited by L. V. Wall, G. A. White, and A. R. Philpott.

The whole of the acting area should be used, not only the front edge of the stage (playboard). Puppets should not appear from below except when the action demands this, as, for instance, when a character has to come up from a cellar or underground cavern. The effect of a fish leaping out of water and returning with a splash, or of some magical character slowly arising out of the ground, will be much more impressive if the other characters enter and exit through the normal places provided.

THE PRODUCTION

One of the main functions of the producer is the ensuring of clear, unobstructed view for the audience by checking this from various positions in the auditorium. Usually the spectators are looking slightly upwards at the puppets, and it will be noticed that puppets retreating from the front edge of the stage appear to be going slightly "downhill". This effect is

PUPPET PLAY PRODUCTION

counteracted by slightly increasing their playing height as they go towards the backscreen. When puppets enter, too, they should be held well up to the top of the doorway, or they will not be fully visible.

The arms of performers, especially if they are children, will tend at first to tire quickly, and the puppets will tend to drop partly out of sight. This is one reason for having plenty of movement, with characters coming and going, not standing in one position making long speeches.

Normally, only the puppet which is speaking should be moving, emphasizing his remarks with head and hand movements. There can, of course, be exceptions, for which there will be good dramatic reasons, and there may be crowd action at times. It will, however, become almost impossible for the audience to tell which are the speaking characters if a number of puppets are bobbing around simultaneously. Attention is distracted by meaningless movement.

As in the "live" theatre, the stage should not be left empty for any length of time, or there will be risk of the thread of interest being broken. If there is the occasional and *intentional* gap, for the purpose of building up dramatic tension, this will require precise timing.

If much of the action has to take place offstage, according to the script, then that play is probably inherently unsuitable. An audience wants to *see* the hero kill the dragon, rescue the princess; it does not want the hero merely to enter and *say* he has done these deeds elsewhere!

To ensure the essential continuity of performance adequate rehearsal is needed, particularly in regard to technical matters. A lively production leaves some degree of flexibility for improvisation within the frame-

xiii

work of the play. There must be backstage organisation to ensure that no puppet, no stage property—or even a puppeteer—is missing at some vital moment, and to ensure that the whole production goes smoothly and at the right tempo.

ACTOR-SPEAKERS

Performers should speak through their puppets and should direct their voices forwards towards the audience. Perfect synchronisation of speech and action is only obtained when the manipulator is also the speaker—and to have an additional performer to do the speaking, or (worse) read the lines, divorcing the speech from the puppet, can be catastrophic. Separate speakers also reduce the backstage space.

A hand puppet can establish an intimate relationship with the audience. A young audience will openly participate and may even influence the development of a play. This is a further reason for *not* having separate speakers, as these may react differently to the manipulators at moments of "audience participation". A really convincing performance, in which the puppets themselves seem to be acting and speaking, is achieved when each performer listens intently to the various characters and watches all the puppets all the time. This is the key secret of effective timing of speech and action.

Usually, the less an audience is aware of the human actors behind the puppets the better. There *can* be points at which the intrusion of human beings may be necessary. With the open-type stage, an audience will accept a visible human hand fixing a tree in position, and there will be no break in continuity as when curtains have to be drawn for scene changes. However, scene shifting can often be done very effectively *by the puppets themselves*.

PROPS

Stage properties can add to the action possibilities of puppet plays. Props need to be (a) clearly visible to the audience in the back row; (b) easily and securely handled by the puppets. When the postman delivers a parcel, it must immediately be clear that this large and exciting package is an important ingredient in the plot. If it is so large that it sticks in the doorway, this will emphasize the point and may lead to amusing stage business.

A prop such as a key may be realistic in its proportion to the size of box to be opened, but may then be too small to be visible when held by the puppet, and easily dropped. There can, of course, be props which are small for good dramatic reasons.

PLAYING TIMES

The climax of a puppet play is usually reached more quickly than that of an equivalent "live" production, and it has been observed that the maximum length for a puppet play to hold the interest of an audience of children is from twenty to thirty minutes. However, no precise time has been indicated for any of the plays in this book, as it is hoped that each producer will feel free to extend, cut, change, according to working conditions, number of performers, and so on. With an audience of young children, their spontaneous "participation" can add five or ten minutes to the anticipated running time of a play.

THE AUDIENCE

An important element in any form of entertainment is the audience. Before presenting a puppet play, the producer should consider the choice of an audience. This may sound an absurdity, as there is never a lack of an audience for a puppet play, but it is essential that the average age of the spectators should bear some relation to the programme presented. Older children at a performance essentially for a younger age group may be audibly sarcastic about a play they consider "too young", and a young audience will become restless if the play is beyond their understanding.

The size of the audience is also of great importance. No matter where they are sitting, everyone should be able to see the puppets in action. It is best to keep the intimacy of the puppet theatre by limiting the number in the audience to the number able to see clearly and in comfort. The producer must, as pointed out elsewhere, study the "sight lines" *from the audience point of view*. A firm estimate should be made of the seating capacity, consistent with good viewing, and admission restricted to this maximum. The show can be repeated if there is an overflow!

If the hall floor is level, not sloping, then the puppet stage should be raised sufficiently for all rows of the audience to be able to see comfortably. Small children should be in the front rows, but these rows should not be too near the stage as the angle of vision would result in tired necks. Action towards the back of the stage would also be out of sight.

Children are probably too young to attend the show if they are too young to sit in the front rows without parents.

THE AUDIENCE

If part of an audience becomes restless because it cannot see properly, or for any other reason, it will disturb the rest of the audience as well as the performers. Producers must study audiences!

THE PLAYS

PUNCH AND THE HEARTLESS GIANT

by LUKE GERTLER

The suitability of the traditional puppet play of *Punch and Judy* for child audiences has been the subject of much discussion in recent years. In *Punch and the Heartless Giant* we see our old friend Punch in a new and less bloodthirsty adventure, said by the author to be "very freely adapted from a fairy tale". It has been performed both as a solo item and by a group of children, average age 12 years.

Characters: Punch
Judy
Princess Golden-Eyes
The Heartless Giant
Quark the Crow
Daphne the Fish
Wilfred the Wolf
A Worm (the original was made from a piece of chest-expander elastic about 12″ long, which stretched when pulled by Quark—the other end being held below-stage by a spare hand).

Properties: Letter
Mattress
Bottle of Orange Juice
String of Sausages (a long thin bag of stocking material, stuffed and tied at intervals with strong thread to form separate sausages.
Key—at least 6″ long
Egg—a cardboard Easter Egg, large enough to contain a good-sized heart and opening into two halves.

EIGHT PLAYS FOR HAND PUPPETS

Heart—(the original was cut from a red rubber sponge. It must fit easily into the egg but must be large enough to be handled easily by a puppet).

Scenes: 1. In Punch's house.
           2. Near a pond.
           3. In the Giant's castle.
           4. By a church.

PUNCH AND THE HEARTLESS GIANT

SCENE 1   *In Punch's House*   (*Enter Punch*)

PUNCH: This wife of mine, Judy, she's always nagging
me. Just listen to her.
  (*Shrill, inaudible words are heard from behind stage,
ending with* " . . . if you don't look out!") What did
I tell you! She carries on like that all day long. Just
to be spiteful I'll sing a little song to annoy her. (*He
begins singing and is interrupted by further threats ending
with* " . . . if you don't stop that row").
  (*Enter Judy*).

JUDY: I can't hear myself think, back in the kitchen.
I've put the gravy on the apple-pie and the custard
on the potatoes, so don't blame me if the dinner
doesn't taste nice.

PUNCH (*Aside*): I'm sure it won't taste any different
from usual.

JUDY (*Shrieking*): What's that you're muttering?

PUNCH: Oh, nothing, dear.

JUDY (*Moving towards the door*): Well, I hope you're
not going to start singing again. It sounds awful.

PUNCH: Oh, so my voice sounds awful, does it! It
doesn't sound half as ghastly as yours when you
learnt singing with that Giovanni Stephano fellow.

JUDY (*Coming back*): It wasn't ghastly; it was jolly nice.
You just listen. (*She begins to sing in a high, shrill,
quivering voice.* PUNCH *blocks his ears*).

PUNCH (*Painfully*): Please don't torture me any more.
It's worse than ever.

JUDY (*Furiously*): Oh, so it's worse than ever, is it! You
just wait, you big . . . (*A knock is heard*). That will be
the postman. I'll go and get the letters. (*Exit Judy*).

4   EIGHT PLAYS FOR HAND PUPPETS

PUNCH: Pfew! I was in for it then. The postman came just in time. (*Re-enter Judy holding a letter*).

JUDY: There's a letter for you, Punch.

PUNCH: Goodness! It has the royal seal on it. It must be from the king. I wonder what's inside?

JUDY: The best way to find out is to open it and read it. Isn't it?

PUNCH: All right, don't snap! (*They open the letter*).

PUNCH (*Reading*): "Dear Punch, My . . . er . . . D-A-U . . . er . . .

JUDY (*Snatching the letter away from* PUNCH): Oh, you're hopeless. Let me read it. (*Reading very fast and without a break:*) "Dear Punch, My daughter, the beautiful golden-eyed Princess, has been kidnapped by the heartless Giant. I would be very grateful if . . . "

PUNCH (*Snatching the letter back from* JUDY): Hey! Wait a minute, Judy, you're reading it so fast that I can't understand a word.

JUDY (*Snatching the letter away from* PUNCH *again*): All right. I'll read it slower this time.

"Dear Punch. My daughter, the beautiful golden-eyed Princess, has been kidnapped by the heartless Giant. I would be very grateful if you would rescue her. If you succeed you will be handsomely rewarded. Signed . . . The King." Oh, Punch! You might get a bag of gold like last time. I'll be able to buy an electric cooker, a washing machine, a television set, a . . .

PUNCH: Stop that, Judy; you musn't hope too much. We haven't got the money yet. Anyway, I don't know whether I ought to go. I don't like the sound of that giant.

JUDY: Don't be so silly; of course you're going. I'll get some things you'll need to take with you. (*She goes out*

PUNCH AND THE HEARTLESS GIANT   5

and returns with a mattress). I thought you might like to take this in case you have to spend the night in a field.

PUNCH: Oh, no, Judy! I can't carry a thing like that all over the countryside.

JUDY: I was only trying to help. (*She goes out again and returns with a bottle of orange juice*). I thought you might be thirsty, so I've got you this.

PUNCH: Not orange juice! What I like is a nice bottle of beer.

JUDY: Well, you're not getting it, so there! You are fussy! (*A short pause*) Ah, I know what you're certain to like! (*She goes out again*).

PUNCH: Now what, I wonder? (*Re-enter* JUDY *with a string of sausages*) Ah, sausages! That's what I like. (*He takes the sausages and moves towards the door*) I'd better be going now. Goodbye, Judy.

JUDY: Goodby, Punch. (*A short pause*) Punch!

PUNCH: What is it, Judy?

JUDY: Haven't you forgotten something?

PUNCH: No, what?

JUDY (*Turning away from him*): You haven't kissed me goodbye.

PUNCH (*Coming back and putting down his sausages*): I'm awfully sorry. Here's a nice big kiss for you. (*He gives her a noisy kiss*).

JUDY (*Weeping*): I didn't mean to nag you all day long as I did.

PUNCH (*Putting his arm around her*): That's all right, Judy. I didn't really mind.

JUDY: And you will take care of yourself, won't you, Punch? You never know what that Giant might do to you.

PUNCH: Don't worry. I'll look after myself. Goodbye! (*He picks up his sausages and goes out*).

6   EIGHT PLAYS FOR HAND PUPPETS

JUDY: Oh, dear! I do hope that nothing happens to
  him. Well, I'd better be getting back to the kitchen.
  The dinner must be all burnt by now. (*She goes out*).

                          SCENE 2

(*Near a Pond. A Willow Tree stands on the Left, about one
third of the length of the stage from the end. Enter a Worm, at
the foot of the tree. He wriggles across the stage to the right,
stopping once to stare at the audience. When he reaches the
right hand side of the stage he begins to descend slowly, his
tail in the air. Enter Quark the Crow*).

QUARK: Lovely day today. I wonder if there are any
  nice fat juicy worms around? (*He catches sight of
  WORM's tail, which is about to disappear*) Ah, there's a
  lively one. (*He grabs the worm's tail and begins to pull*)
  Hard work, this! (*He goes on pulling, but WORM is
  stronger. He pulls QUARK down. Suddenly QUARK's
  wing appears to be caught*). Help! I'm caught in a trap,
  I can't get my wing free! Please help me, somebody.
  (*Enter PUNCH with his sausages*).
PUNCH: Hello! What's going on here?
QUARK: Please get me out; my wing is stuck in this
  trap.
PUNCH: Caught in a trap, eh! (*He peers down*) A nasty
  one with metal teeth.
QUARK: Well, don't just stare. Get me out!
PUNCH (*Pulling QUARK's wing*): This is difficult! (*He
  tries again*) Oh, dear! It looks as if its stuck for good.
  I'll give it a really hard pull this time. Ah! There
  we are!
QUARK: Thank you! I'm free at last. If you want me
  to help you, just call me three times: Quark, Quark,
  Quark!

PUNCH AND THE HEARTLESS GIANT

PUNCH: Like this? Quark, Quark, Quark!

QUARK: That'll do. Goodbye.

PUNCH: Goodbye. (QUARK *flies off*) I'll certainly need some help when I get to the Giant's castle. This is my lucky day. (*He falls in the trap*) Help, help, I'm stuck. Now what did that bird tell me to say? Ah yes! Quark, Quark, Quark! (*Enter* QUARK).

QUARK: You did get into trouble quickly. You are clumsy. Let me get you out. There! Lucky you weren't so stuck as I was. Goodbye! (*He flies off*)

PUNCH: I was stupid to fall in that trap. It'll teach me a lesson. Well, I must be getting along. Hullo! What's this pond? (*He goes over to the tree and looks down.* DAPHNE, *the fish jumps out of the water and hits* PUNCH *on the nose*).

DAPHNE: I beg your pardon. (*She disappears again*).

PUNCH: Goodness! What on earth was that? (DAPHNE *appears again, and starts jumping in and out of the pond. Suddenly she makes a bigger leap than before and lands with her head hanging over the front of the stage*).

DAPHNE: Help, help, I'm drowning! I can't breathe any more. Help, I'm dying . . . (*She faints*).

PUNCH: She surely is in a bad way. I'd better put her back in the water. There! Now I'll just wait a minute until she recovers. (*A pause.* DAPHNE *re-appears*).

DAPHNE: Oh, thank you! Thank you so much! You have saved my life!

PUNCH: What exactly happened?

DAPHNE: I was doing my morning exercises. I jumped too high into the air and instead of landing back in the water I landed on the edge; and if you hadn't put me back into my dear pond I would have been drowned for certain.

8 EIGHT PLAYS FOR HAND PUPPETS

PUNCH: What do you mean? You only drown in water.

DAPHNE: Only you humans drown in water. We fish drown when we are *out* of it. If you want me to help you when you are in trouble just call my name three times: Daphne, Daphne, Daphne!

PUNCH: Like this? Daphne, Daphne, Daphne?

DAPHNE: That's right. Goodbye!

PUNCH: Goodbye. (DAPHNE *dives into the pond*) I did like that fish. She was ever so nice. Now I've got two friends to help me. (*Groans are heard off-stage*) Oh dear! What's that? Sounds like someone else in trouble. (*Enter* WILFRED THE WOLF).

WILFRED (*Weakly*): Oh dear, oh me! I'm so hungry! I haven't eaten anything for seven days, ten hours and twenty minutes, and I'm so weak that I can hardly walk. (*He flops over the front of the stage*).

PUNCH: Dear me! He looks starved, the poor thing.

WILFRED: If you don't give me something to eat quickly, I'll die.

PUNCH: Well, If I give you my sausages I'll die of hunger myself.

WILFRED: Oh, no you won't. Because if I eat something I'll be strong again, and I'll be able to take you anywhere, on my back, to where there's more food.

PUNCH: All right, then. I'll give them to you. (*He helps the* WOLF *to stand up, but the* WOLF *falls down again*) Oh, dear, he's too weak to stand up. I'll have to prop him up against the tree. That's better. (*He gives* WILFRED *the sausages*).

WILFRED (*Brightly*): Ah! I feel strong again now. Thank you kindly. Where would you like me to take you?

PUNCH AND THE HEARTLESS GIANT   9

PUNCH: I'm on my way to the castle of the Heartless
Giant to rescue the princess Golden-Eyes.

WILFRED: I can't possibly take you there. It's far too
dangerous. Oh, dear me, no. Never, never, never!

PUNCH: Can't you just take me within a mile of the
castle? I'll walk the rest of the way.

WILFRED: Very well, then. But I won't take you any
nearer than a mile. Hop on my back before I change
my mind. (PUNCH *climbs on to* WILFRED's *back. The
two go off*).

SCENE 3 (*in the Giant's Castle. Enter Princess Golden-Eyes*).

PRINCESS: Woe is me! I'm so unhappy. I have been
captured by the Heartless Giant and there is no
hope of escape. I have to cook for him, mend his
clothes, do all the washing and ironing. It's hardly
the right thing for a princess to be doing. I wish
some handsome prince would come and rescue me.
Hark! I hear footsteps. (*She looks out of the door*) It's
not a prince. (*She looks again*) And he's not handsome
either. (*Enter* PUNCH). Why! It's Mr. Punch from
my home town. I am glad to see you.

PUNCH: Your father, the King, sent me a letter and
asked me to rescue you. Which is the best way to
escape?

PRINCESS: The Giant has put a spell on me which
stops me from leaving his castle. The only way to
break that spell would be to find his heart. He keeps
it carefully hidden, and nobody but himself knows
where it is kept.

PUNCH: Perhaps you could find out somehow.

PRINCESS: I'll try to get him to tell me when he comes
in. He's gone to chop some wood. He'll be back any
time now. (*Loud singing is heard*). Here he is. Go

10   EIGHT PLAYS FOR HAND PUPPETS

quickly and hide in the cellar. (*Exit* PUNCH) Oh
dear, I do hope that the Giant doesn't see him.
(*Enter* GIANT).

GIANT: I smell the blood of an Englishman.

PRINCESS: It's only your dinner cooking in the oven.

GIANT: Oh, is that all. You remember that forest
which stood behind the castle?

PRINCESS: Yes.

GIANT: It doesn't stand any longer. I've chopped it all
down.

PRINCESS: You are strong, Mr. Giant. (*She lowers her
head*).

GIANT: Why are you looking so sad, my little princess?

PRINCESS: It's so difficult for me to love you when I
haven't got your heart.

GIANT: Ah! So you want my heart, do you? It's so well
hidden that no one could ever find it.

PRINCESS: Please, please tell me where it lies; it would
make me so happy.

GIANT: Well, I don't see any harm in telling you. It's
hidden under the front door mat.

PRINCESS: Thank you a thousand times, Mr. Giant.

GIANT: No trouble, my dear, no trouble at all. Now I
must be off to fetch the forest that I've just cut down
into our back yard. Goodbye. (*Exit* GIANT).

PRINCESS: He does keep his heart in a funny place. It's
funny that I've never noticed it there before, when
I sweep out the hall. (*Moving to the door*) You can
come up now, Mr. Punch. The Giant has gone.
(*Enter* PUNCH).

PUNCH: Did you find out where he keeps his heart?

PRINCESS: Yes, he says it's under the front door mat.

PUNCH (*Laughing*): He-he! It must be squashed flat by
now. I'll go and fetch it. (*He goes out*).

PUNCH AND THE HEARTLESS GIANT 11

PRINCESS: I do hope it really is there. (*Re-enter* PUNCH).

PUNCH: I can't find it.

PRINCESS: Oh, dear, the Giant has tricked me. Go and hide again, and I'll get him to tell me the truth when he comes back; and on your way out, put some flowers on the front door mat.

PUNCH: Flowers on the front door mat? What ever for?

PRINCESS: Never mind what for. Go quickly, I can hear the Giant coming. (*Exit* PUNCH) When the Giant sees the flowers, he'll think that I still believe that his heart is hidden underneath the mat. (*Enter* GIANT).

GIANT: All the forest I've chopped down is now lying in the back yard.

PRINCESS: That is clever of you, Mr. Giant.

GIANT: By the way, what on earth are those flowers lying about on the front doormat?

PRINCESS: Can't you guess, my dear Mr. Giant? It's because it's the place where your heart lies.

GIANT (*Laughing loudly*): Ho-ho! So you really think that I would be stupid enough to keep it there? Well, I lied to you. It's not there at all.

PRINCESS: You are unkind. I'm so unhappy again.

GIANT: So you really want to know where it lies?

PRINCESS: Oh, yes, more than anything in the world.

GIANT: All right then, I'll tell you. It's under my pillow in the bedroom. And now I've got to chop all the wood into tiny pieces so that your delicate little hands can fit them in the kitchen stove to cook my lambs. Cheerio! (*He goes out*).

PRINCESS: That's another funny place for him to keep his heart. I might as well look.
(*She goes out and comes back after a short pause*) The Giant has lied to me again; his heart is not there.

Anyway, I've put flowers on his pillow. (*Enter* GIANT).

GIANT: I've chopped all the wood up for you. You'll have enough to last you the whole winter.

PRINCESS: That is kind of you. I've put some flowers on your pillow.

GIANT: What on earth for? Oh, I see! You think my heart is hidden under it. (*He laughs*) Well, I lied to you again.

PRINCESS (*Weeping*): Oh, you are cruel. Please, please tell me the truth. It would make me so happy.

GIANT: Well, as you really want to know, I'll tell you. Far, far away in a distant land there is a lake. In the middle of that lake, there is an island. On that island there stands a church. By that church there stands a well. In that well there swims a duck. In that duck there lies an egg, and in that egg lies my heart. No one could possibly find it. My hiding place is far too good. Well, I must go and put all the wood in the barn. Goodbye. (*He goes out*).

PRINCESS: At last, I feel sure that he told me the truth. It sounds far too good to be another lie. (*She goes to the door*) Mr. Punch, come quickly. I know where the heart really is. (*Enter* PUNCH).

PUNCH: That's marvellous. Tell me quickly and I'll go and fetch it straight away.

PRINCESS: Now listen carefully. It's rather complicated. In some distant land there is a lake; in the lake there is an island; on the island stands a church, and by the church there stands a well; in the well swims a duck; in the duck lies an egg; and finally in the egg lies the Giant's heart.

PUNCH: Pfew! I hope I can remember all that. I'll go quickly before the Giant comes back again. You'll

PUNCH AND THE HEARTLESS GIANT

be free very soon now, Princess Golden-Eyes. Goodbye!

PRINCESS: Goodbye. Look after yourself. (PUNCH *goes out*) Soon I'll be back in my father's castle.

GIANT'S voice: I want my dinner!

PRINCESS: All right, I'm coming. (*She goes out*).

SCENE 4 (*By a Church. The top of a well is just visible. Enter* PUNCH).

PUNCH: I've reached the church at last. Now what did the Princess say? "By the church stands a well". This must be it. Oh, dear! There's a door across the top, and it's locked. I'll see if the key is inside the church. (*He enters the church and comes out again after a pause*) It's hanging right at the very top, on the inside of the steeple. I can't possibly reach it. I'll call Quark the Crow. He'll be able to fly up to it. Quark, Quark, Quark! (*Enter* QUARK).

QUARK: Hello! In trouble again?

PUNCH: Yes. Could you please fetch me the key which is hanging high up inside the church?

QUARK: I won't be a minute. (*He flies into the church and returns with the key*).

PUNCH: Thanks ever so much.

QUARK: I've done my job, so I must be off. Goodbye!

PUNCH: Goodbye, Quark, and thanks again. (*Exit* QUARK). Now let's have a look inside the well. (*He unlocks the well and looks down*) There's a duck right at the bottom. The princess said, "In the well there swims a duck, and in the duck there lies an egg". To get the egg I shall have to catch the duck, and the duck is too far down to reach. I'll call that nice fish. She will help me. Daphne, Daphne, Daphne! (DAPHNE *appears from the well*).

C

14 EIGHT PLAYS FOR HAND PUPPETS

DAPHNE: Can I do anything for you, Mr. Punch?

PUNCH: Yes, please, Daphne. You know that old duck at the bottom of the well?

DAPHNE: Of course I do. I've known him for years.

PUNCH: Could you ask him for the egg he keeps hidden inside him?

DAPHNE: He's a very bad-tempered old duck, you know. But I'll do my best. (DAPHNE *disappears and returns with a large egg*).

PUNCH: Oh, you've got it, Daphne! In that egg lies the Giant's heart. Will you help me open it? (*They open the egg; a heart falls out.* PUNCH *touches the heart and a loud yell is heard*).

DAPHNE: Oh, dear! I don't like this heart very much; it's too noisy. I'd better go home and leave you to do what you like with it. Goodbye.

PUNCH: Goodbye Daphne, and thank you for being so kind. (*He gives her a little kiss on the nose.* DAPHNE *gives a squeak of delight and disappears*).

PUNCH: Ah! Now that I've got the Giant's heart at last, I can make him do anything I like. I'll see if he can feel this. (*He gives the heart a little squeeze. Another loud yell is heard*).

GIANT'S Voice: Whoever it is, please don't touch my heart; it hurts!

PUNCH: I won't leave it alone until you have done exactly what I tell you.

GIANT'S Voice: I'll do anything you want as long as you don't squeeze my heart.

PUNCH: Then release the Princess Golden-Eyes.

GIANT'S Voice: Very well. I'm going to throw her right across the world to where you are. You'll have to wait a little for her arrival. (*Sadly*) Off you go my little princess. (*A pause. Princess sails in and droops over the front*).

PUNCH AND THE HEARTLESS GIANT

PRINCESS (*Getting up*): What's happened to me? How did I get here?

PUNCH: The Giant threw you across the world. Are you feeling all right?

PRINCESS: Yes, thank you. I am glad to see you, Mr. Punch. You really have rescued me. You don't think that wicked Giant can get us any more?

PUNCH: I'll just make sure (*He gives the heart a tiny squeeze—another yell*) Mr. Giant, do you promise to behave yourself in future and to stop kidnapping princesses?

GIANT's Voice: Yes, yes, I promise.

PUNCH: Because if you don't behave I'll squeeze your heart really hard.

GIANT's Voice: I'll be a good giant now, so never squeeze my heart again.

PUNCH (*To Princess*): Just in case he breaks his promise, I'll keep his heart. Shall we go home now? Judy must be getting very worried.

PRINCESS: Yes, let's go home. I'm longing to see my dear father again.

PUNCH (*To audience*): Goodbye, everybody.

PRINCESS: Goodbye.

(*They go off*)

THE END

OWL'S BIRTHDAY

by Pantopuck the Puppetman

This is an original play. It can be performed by one person or by a group. There are no changes of scenery.

Characters: Owl
Squirrel
Bear
Mouse
Tortoise
Toady, who lives under a toadstool (His hair looks very much like Squirrel's tail).

Properties: Bar of Chocolate in gaudy wrapper
Green Honeypot
Bell-pull (i.e. a chain suspended from the foliage of the tree, with a large ring at the bottom for pulling. A real bell off-stage is rung by hand.
Silver Bauble (such as a ball from a Christmas tree)
Cheese
Butterfly net.

OWL'S BIRTHDAY

SCENE: *A sturdy oak tree, with a small house in the foliage, with the word OWL over its window; a large hole in the lower part of the trunk, curtained, this being the Larder. To one side, at front of stage, a gay toadstool, like a seat. Some bright green grass along the front.*

(*Enter* SQUIRREL. *Squirrel explores the area, with quick movements and short pauses, perhaps dropping nutshells. Then goes out.*)

(*Enter* TORTOISE *chanting* HUMP, HUMP; HUMP, HUMP; *etc. and carrying a bar of chocolate, with gay wrapper. Tortoise places the chocolate centre-front and eyes the tree*).

(*Enter* BEAR *carrying a green honeypot*) Hello, Tortoise!

TORTOISE: Hello, Bear!

BEAR: What have you got there, Tortoise?

TORTOISE: Chocolate!

BEAR: What's that for?

TORTOISE: It's Owly's birthday present.

BEAR: Oh! Is it his birthday today?

TORTOISE: Yes.

BEAR: Perhaps *I* ought to get him a birthday present.

TORTOISE: Yes, perhaps you should.

BEAR (*Thinks* . . .): I know, I've got a nice silver ball at home. Perhaps he would like that!

TORTOISE: Yes, perhaps he would.

BEAR: I'll go and get it.

TORTOISE: You have to sing a little song, Bear.

BEAR: Do I? Which one, Tortoise?

TORTOISE: It goes "Happy birthday to you, Happy birthday to you . . ."

18 EIGHT PLAYS FOR HAND PUPPETS

BEAR: All right, Tortoise, I'll try and remember it!
Goodbye!

TORTOISE: Goodbye, Bear! (*Exit* BEAR *singing quietly
. . . .*) And now I had better ring the bell and give
Owly his chocolate.

OWL (*As the bell rings*): Who's that ringing my bell . . .
(*Quickly*) and-waking-me-up-on-my-birthday! (*Opens
window*).

TORTOISE: It's only me, Tortoise. I've brought you
some chocolate for your birthday.

OWL: I don't want to be wakened up on my birthday!

TORTOISE: I'm sorry! What shall I do with the chocolate?

OWL: Put in in my larder. (TORTOISE *starts singing as
he puts the chocolate in the tree—but* OWL *slams the
window shut before the song reaches its end*).

TORTOISE: Well! He's a grumpy, growly, Owly on his
birthday, isn't he! Oh, well! (*Exit* TORTOISE, *with
a HUMP, HUMP;*) (*Enter* BEAR *practising the song
quietly, carrying silver bauble*) (*Enter* MOUSE) Hello,
Bear!

BEAR: Hello, Mouse!

MOUSE: What have you got there, Bear?

BEAR: It's a birthday present for Owly.

MOUSE: Is it his birthday today?

BEAR: Yes, Mouse.

MOUSE: Perhaps *I* should get him a present.

BEAR: Yes, perhaps you should, Mouse.

MOUSE: Perhaps I could find him a nice piece of
cheese.

BEAR: That's a good idea, Mouse.

MOUSE: I'll go and look, Bear.

BEAR: You have to sing a little song, Mouse.

MOUSE: Which one, Bear?

OWL'S BIRTHDAY

BEAR: Oh, dear, I've forgotten!

MOUSE: I remember, Bear, it goes: "Happy birthday to you . . ."

BEAR: That's it, Mouse. Thank you! I'd better ring the bell . . .

MOUSE: And I'll go and find some cheese. . . . (*Exit* MOUSE).

BEAR: (*Rings the bell*).

OWL: Who's that ringing my bell and (*Quickly*) waking-me-up-on-my-birthday?

BEAR: It's only Bear. I've brought you a nice present.

OWL (*Opening window*): I don't want to be wakened on my birthday!

BEAR: What shall I do with it, Owly?

OWL: Put it in my larder.

BEAR (*Starts to sing, puts bauble in the tree, but Owl has slammed the window in the middle of the singing . . .*) Well, he's a grumpy Owly on his birthday, isn't he! (*Exit singing quietly*) (*Enter* MOUSE *carrying large piece of cheese wrapped in cellophane*) *As he enters, the Toadstool suddenly leans over on a hinge, and* TOADY, *whose hair is just like the* SQUIRREL'S *tail, emerges.* MOUSE *hides.* TOADY *looks about to see if all clear and then peeps into* OWL'S *larder and takes out the silver bauble. He does not speak, but shows his delight by dumb-show, then disappears in his hole and the toadstool resumes original position*).

MOUSE (*Reappearing and placing cheese centre-front*): Oh! Owly won't like that! I must ring the bell and tell him.

OWL (*As bell begins to ring*): Who's that ringing my bell —and waking-me-up-on-my-birthday?

MOUSE: It's Mouse! Owly, I think I saw Squirrel taking one of your presents!

EIGHT PLAYS FOR HAND PUPPETS

OWL: Which one?

MOUSE: It was a silver ball.

OWL: My best present! You must go and tell Bear at once, and tell him to get it back for me.

MOUSE: All right, Owly! I've brought you a present.

OWL: Well, put it in my larder.

MOUSE (*Starting to sing* "Happy Birthday", *puts cheese in larder, but* OWL *has already slammed shut the window, muttering about being woken up . . .*).

BEAR (*Heard off-stage, asking* MOUSE "Which way do we go?*).

MOUSE (*Entering*): This way, Bear.

BEAR: Which way did Squirrel go, Mouse?

MOUSE: He went over by that Toadstool, Bear.

BEAR: Let's have a look for footprints.

MOUSE: Here's one.

BEAR: Here's another.

MOUSE: And here's another one.

BEAR: That's funny! There aren't any more!

MOUSE (*Looks under the seat of the toadstool*): Even Squirrel can't *fly*!

BEAR (*Sits on edge of the Toadstool, which moves slightly. He gets off, examines it, sits down again. Again it moves a little*): That's funny! Must be somebody underneath. I know, Mouse! I'll go and get my butterfly net and see if I can catch him.

MOUSE: That's a good idea, Bear. But I must be going. Goodbye!

BEAR: Goodbye, Mouse, and thank you! (BEAR *and* MOUSE *go off in opposite directions. But in a group show* MOUSE *could stay with* BEAR, *and join in the capture of* TOADY).

OWL'S BIRTHDAY

BEAR (*Reappearing with net*): Nobody about yet! (*He sits on the Toadstool more heavily, it heaves, he steps away as* TOADY *emerges*). Oh it's *you*, Toady! (*Chases* TOADY *and catches him in net*). What do you mean by taking Owly's birthday present?

TOADY: Well, he shouldn't be such a grumpy, growly, Owly on his birthday.

BEAR: You still shouldn't take his birthday present, the one *I* gave him too! Go and get it back this minute!

TOADY: All right. Let me out!

BEAR (*Removing net*): Hurry up! And don't you ever go taking other people's birthday presents again!

TOADY (*Dives down hole, re-emerges with the bauble*): Here you are!

BEAR: Thank you. And don't forget—never take other people's birthday presents again.

TOADY: Well, he *shouldn't* be such a . . . (*He dives below and pulls the Toadstool over him as* BEAR *swings the net again*).

BEAR: Well, he *was* a grumpy, growly, Owly—but it *was* his birthday. I had better ring the bell and give him his present again. (*Rings . . .*).

OWL: Who's that ringing my bell—and waking-me-up-on-my birthday? (*Opens window*). Oh, it's you again.

BEAR: I've got your birthday present back for you.

OWL: I'll come down and have a look at it (*Flies in*).

BEAR: Here you are, Owly.

OWL: Thank you, Bear. I'm sorry I was so grumpy growly—but I only want to *sleep* all day on my birthday.

BEAR: Never mind, Owly.

22   EIGHT PLAYS FOR HAND PUPPETS

OWL: I know! We'll have a birthday party in the woods on Saturday, Bear. You go and tell all the animals.

BEAR: That's a nice idea, Owly. They'll like that! I'll go right away. Goodbye, Owly!

OWL: Goodbye Bear. And now I can go back to sleep. (*Exit* BEAR *singing happily.* "*Happy birthday to you . . .*")

(*The last we hear of* OWL *is a contented snore . . .*)

THE END

Introduction to THE SILVER KEY

The origins of this play are well-documented. We can see the early stages of its growth as illustrating our general remarks on the building of a play.

A class of children was asked to write a story. To help them, the following was written on the blackboard:

A Postman delivers a box to Pete. On it is written:
"Unlock me with the silver key
And treasure you will find.
Get the key from the owl in the oak
Which grows in a wood near the wizard's smoke."
Here are some characters to help you write a story which could be used for writing a puppet play:
Postman, Pete, Pete's Mother, Hermit, Badger, Wizard, Witch, Bear, Owl, Laughing Jack.

The suggested characters were carefully chosen. Pete was the hero. (In the final version of the play, we find that he has changed his name to Danny, "because Pete didn't sound right").

Like most small boys Pete had a Mother. The Hermit suggests a wise person to go to for advice.

The Witch and the Wizard add a touch of excitement and magic, while Bear and Badger were suggested for animal interest. The Owl fitted in with the rhyme, and, like the Hermit, suggests a fairly benevolent wisdom.

Out of the batch of stories which resulted from this exercise, the following was chosen as the basis for the play. It was written by a girl of 11 years.

STORY :

Early one morning when Pete was helping his mother do the housework, he heard a knock on the door. It was the postman, but today instead of bringing letters he had a large parcel. Joyfully Pete took it and thanked the postman. Very quickly he undid the paper round it and to his amazement he found a large box with a label on it saying:

Unlock me with the silver key

And treasure you will find.

Get the key from the owl in the oak

Which grows in a wood near the wizard's smoke.

When Pete had read this message, he went to see his friend Dan and his sister Joan. After he had told them about the message they were very, very willing to join his adventure.

The nearest wood to where they lived was about a mile away, but as it was a bright day they decided to walk there. It was about half an hour before they arrived, and there by the entrance of the wood sat a hermit who was smoking a long pipe. The children asked him if a wizard lived in the wood and the hermit answered in a gruff tone that one lived in a hut by the oak tree. The hermit offered to take them there and the children agreed.

When they arrived at the wizard's hut they saw a large bear guarding the entrance. Close by him stood a tall man who named himself Laughing Jack. He told them that the wizard was in one of his fits of killing every person he saw, so the bear had to guard him. At that moment Laughing Jack and the bear were carried

INTRODUCTION TO THE SILVER KEY

inside the hut by two black hands. The children were running away when suddenly a badger came out from a bush and said "Are you looking for the oak tree, because it's over there?" and vanished again.

The oak tree was very broad round the trunk and up in the topmost branches they saw a brown owl. It fluttered down and dropped a package into Pete's hand. "That is for you", the owl said, and flew back into the topmost branches again.

As they were walking back through the wood two dark shadowy figures pounced out of the growth. "Give us that package," ordered the two, who were the witch and the wizard. Pete told Dan and Joan to run as fast as they could. The witch and wizard gave chase and kept shouting, "Come back, you rogues, come back!" When the children were out of the wood the wizard and witch stopped chasing and the children were able to open the package. Inside it was a silver key that was to open the box.

When the children arrived home they opened the box and inside it was a casket of white powder and a note saying that if you should sprinkle this on the badger, bear and owl, they would all change back to who they were originally.

Again they set off into the wood where they found the three animals. Pete sprinkled the powder on the animals, and they were changed into two princes and a princess.

The children were each given a crisp pound note and they were as happy as ever they could be.

It will be seen that the story and the subsequent play are built around the box and the need for getting the right key with which to open it. When the puppets were made, the story was acted out on the stage. Gradually in the course of rehearsal, the unmanageable parts of the story were dropped, and the plot changed with the flow of ideas, until finally the play settled down into the form in which it was written down.

THE SILVER KEY

by CHILDREN OF A JUNIOR-MIXED SCHOOL

Characters: Danny
Danny's mother
Postman
Witch
Wizard
Owl
A Badger, who turns into a Princess
A Bear, who turns into a Prince
Laughing Jack, who turns into Dog Toby.

Properties: A wooden box, having only 3 sides and an open back into which the puppets can disappear.
Silver key
Whistle
Drum
Pepper pot
Pipe, a flat cut-out of balsa wood. Smoke to be puffed out from it by squeezing a rubber bulb filled with talcum powder.
Postman's sack (attached to Postman)
Scissors (cardboard, silvered).

Scenery: 1. Outside Danny's house.
2. Entrance to Wizard's house.
3. Owl's oak tree.

THE SILVER KEY   27

SCENE 1.   Danny at home.

(DANNY *enters whistling in a spasmodic, lazy manner*).

DANNY: Oh dear! I am bored this morning. I've got nothing at all to do. (*Loud rat-tat on door*). Whatever was that? It startled me. I'll just have a peep outside. (*Peeps round door and returns to say*). It's the postman, but he doesn't usually knock. Perhaps he's got a parcel. (*Opens door and there stands Postman with postbag on his back and box in his hand. The box is tied round with ribbon*).

POSTMAN: Good morning, Danny! I've got a parcel for you.

DANNY: For me? How lovely! It does look exciting. I wonder what's inside it, Postman?

POSTMAN: Well open it, silly, and find out. It certainly is enormous, Danny. But I must be on my way. (POSTMAN *goes out, but pokes his head round door to call out to* DANNY). Tell me what's inside the parcel when I come round tomorrow, Danny.

DANNY: Yes, I will, Postman. Good-bye. (*He struggles in vain with red ribbon*). I know! I'll fetch my scissors. (*Goes out and returns with very large pair of silvered cardboard scissors*). Now I won't be long. Snip. Snip. That's it. (*Ribbon is unfastened from back by a helping hand, as though cut by scissors*). Now I'll see what is in the box. What's this? A label! And some writing on it. Oh, bother! I'm far too excited to read it. (*Calls:*) Mother! Mother! (*Upstairs window slides open and* MOTHER *pops her head out*).

MOTHER: What do you want, Danny? I'm busy making the beds.

DANNY: Please come down, Mother. The Postman has brought me a big parcel, and I'm much too excited to read the label. Do come and read it for me. Please!

MOTHER: Very well, I'll come. Just a moment, Danny. (*She comes in and goes over to box to read label*).
"Unlock me with the silver key
  And treasure you will find.
 Get the key from the owl in the oak
  Which grows in the wood near the wizard's smoke".

DANNY: Oh, Mother! Please let me go into the wood to find this silver key.

MOTHER: Nonsense, Danny! Someone is playing a trick on you. What a lot of nonsense this all is.

DANNY: Please! I'm sure it's not a joke. I'm certain it's really true. Do let me go—*please*! I'll be very careful.

MOTHER (*Hesitantly*): Very well, Danny. But for goodness sake be back home before your father returns tonight. You know what he'll say if you're not here when he comes in.

DANNY: Oh, thank you. (*Kisses* MOTHER *excitedly*). Thank you, thank you, Mother! Goodbye! (*Goes out, turns back at door and calls:*) Goodbye! I'll remember to be back before father gets home. Don't worry. Bye-bye!

MOTHER (*Shakes her head thoughtfully as she goes out*): I do hope he'll be safe and get back before his father comes home.

SCENE 2.   Danny comes to the wood.

(*Enter* HERMIT *walking slowly and stopping to look around to enjoy the wood. He makes his way to the side of the stage and sits down*).

THE SILVER KEY 29

HERMIT: What a beautiful day to be sure. The wood is at its best on such a sunny morning. Now where's my old pipe? Ah! here it is. (*Pipe handed up by concealed hand*). Let's get it going now, then I shall be really happy. (*Mimes lighting of pipe. Concealed hand puffs "talcum smoke" from behind pipe-bowl*). That's it! Now I'll sit here quietly for a while and rest.

(*Whistling heard off stage and* DANNY *enters*). Good morning, boy. What are you doing in my wood?

DANNY: I want to find a silver key, sir. This morning the postman brought me a big box, and on it was a label which said:

"Unlock me with the silver key
 And treasure you will find.
 Get the key from the owl in the oak
 Which grows in the wood near the wizard's
 smoke".

So you see, sir, I must find the key to unlock the box.

HERMIT: Well, you've set yourself a difficult task, boy. First you must get past the witch ... Ummm! mmm! mmm!

DANNY: A witch! Oh dear!

HERMIT: Then you've got to get past the wizard (*shakes his head ominously*). Mm! mm! tut! tut! Mm!

DANNY: A wizard! Oh no!

HERMIT: Yes, boy! The witch lives in a house guarded by a badger, and the wizard's house is guarded by a bear. Do you know, boy, that once, long ago, a Prince and Princess were out in this wood with their dog Toby and they all disappeared? They've never been seen since, boy. Never! Never! (*shakes his head sadly*).

DANNY: But isn't there any chance of my getting past the wizard and the witch, Mr. Hermit?

D

30 EIGHT PLAYS FOR HAND PUPPETS

HERMIT: Well! There's just one chance. If you say this little rhyme—you might—I say you *might* just manage it.

DANNY: What is the rhyme, Mr. Hermit?

HERMIT: Listen, boy.

"Hocum, pocum,
 Tickle or chok'em".

And if you do get past them, the owl's oak tree lies straight ahead of you. Knock three times on the tree and the owl will appear.

DANNY (*To himself*): Hocum pocum . . . Tickle or chok'em. I mustn't forget it. (*To audience*). You'll help me to remember it, won't you? (*Goes out repeating rhyme to himself*).

SCENE 3.   Danny meets with Witch

(BADGER *enters sleepily and snuffles his way along. He settles in a corner, curls up and goes to sleep. Enter* DANNY).

DANNY: Oh! There's the badger and he guards the witch. I must keep very quiet now. Sh! Sh! (*Goes out*).

BADGER (*He wakes up and sniffs very audibly around the stage*): I smell (*Sniff, sniff*) BOY. (*Sniff, sniff, sniff*) I must tell my mistress the witch about this (*Pokes head out of door and calls*). Mistress Witch! Mistress Witch! I smell BOY.

WITCH (*Off stage*): Coming, Badger. Coming! (*A piercing scream, and* WITCH *flies on to stage*). Did you say you smelt Boy, Badger?

BADGER: Yes, Mistress Witch, I did.

WITCH: Where did he go?

BADGER: I don't know. I was asleep, Mistress Witch.

THE SILVER KEY

WITCH: Asleep! You lazy, good-for-nothing Badger. (*To audience*). Do you know where he went?

AUDIENCE: Yes.

WITCH: Good! Will you tell me?

AUDIENCE: No.

WITCH: So you're on his side, are you? I don't care. I'll find him without your help. You see if I don't. (DANNY *pokes his head round door. He sees* WITCH, *exclaims "Ah!" and hurriedly withdraws*).

WITCH: What was that? Was it the Boy?

AUDIENCE: Yes.

WITCH: Right! I'll soon find him. (*Goes out*).

BADGER: Now I'll just finish my little nap in peace. (*Re-enter* WITCH).

WITCH: I can't see Boy, Badger. Are you sure you smelled him?

BADGER: (*Snore, Snore, Snore*).

WITCH (*Shaking* BADGER): Wake up, you lazy old Badger. Did you smell Boy?

BADGER: Yes indeed, but I've got an idea, Mistress Witch. Why don't you go up to your tree-top house and watch from there for the Boy?

WITCH: Jolly good idea, Badger. Here I go! (*Flies out of door and appears through top window*). Ha, ha, ha! Ha, ha ha! I'll catch this wretched Boy now. (*She scans the distant horizon for signs of* DANNY. DANNY *enters, peers round door and whispers*).

DANNY: Hocum Pocum, Tickle or chok'em! (*He creeps along as he says it right under the nose of the* WITCH, *and goes out*).

WITCH: I must have missed him, Badger, but I'll catch him when he returns. Never fear! Ha ha ha! (*She comes down with a piercing scream.* BADGER *and* WITCH *go out*).

32   EIGHT PLAYS FOR HAND PUPPETS

DANNY (*Re-enters*): Thank goodness I'm past the
    witch. She was beastly. Now I must get past the
    wizard, and then I can find the oak tree and the
    silver key. (*Infectious rippling laughter heard off stage*).
    What's that? Someone laughing? (LAUGHING JACK
    enters, continuing with his infectious laughter).

DANNY: What's your name?

LAUGHING JACK: Give me sixpence and I might tell
    you.

DANNY: Here you are then. (*Hands over coin*).

LAUGHING JACK (*Still laughing*): I only said I MIGHT!

DANNY: Silly creature! I can't waste valuable time on
    you. Good-bye! (*Goes out*).

(LAUGHING JACK *goes out still laughing*)

SCENE 4.   In front of Wizard's front door.

(BEAR *enters*).

BEAR: I am the Bear. I guard the Wizard's house like
    this. (*Marches up and down*).
    (WIZARD *enters*).

WIZARD: Good morning, Bear!

BEAR: Good morning, Master Wizard.

WIZARD: You are a lonely bear, aren't you? Would
    you like a companion?

BEAR: I certainly would, Master Wizard.

WIZARD: That's easily arranged. The next living thing
    that passes by I will change into a bear for you.

BEAR: Thank you, Master Wizard.

WIZARD: Now do not disturb me, Bear. I'm going to
    sleep in the sun. (*He goes to sleep and* BEAR *marches up
    and down*). (DANNY *enters*).

BEAR: Halt! Who goes there?

DANNY: It is I. Danny.

THE SILVER KEY

BEAR: What do you want?

DANNY: I want to see the Wizard.

BEAR: Do you, my boy? Well, I'll get him for you. (*Shakes* WIZARD).

WIZARD: I thought I told you not to wake me up, Bear.

BEAR: Yes, Master, you did—but here's a boy wanting to see you.

WIZARD: A boy, eh?

DANNY (*In a shaky voice*): Good morning, Wizard.

WIZARD: Um! Just about the right size for our little plan, don't you think, Bear?

BEAR: Yes, Master.

WIZARD: Yes, I'll change him into a bear.

DANNY: I we— w— w— wonder wh— wh— what's going to h— h— happen to me?

BEAR: Cast your spell, Master Wizard. (DANNY *kneels down in centre of stage and* WIZARD *waves his arms over him.* WIZARD *and* DANNY *both talk at the same time*).

WIZARD: Izzy whizzy, izzy woo,
Make something wonderful happen to you!
Change into a bear.

DANNY: Hocum, Pocum, Tickle or chok'em (*Repeated continuously*). (WIZARD *and* BEAR *watch* DANNY).

WIZARD: That's funny! It hasn't worked. I'll repeat it. (WIZARD *and* DANNY *repeat their spells together again*).

WIZARD: Again my spell has failed. I must go into my study, Bear, and look it up in my Book of Spells. (BEAR *and* WIZARD *go into house*)

DANNY (*Whispering*): Now's my chance. (*Goes out hurriedly*). (WIZARD *and* BEAR *return*).

WIZARD: My spell was quite right. Why! What's the matter, Bear?

BEAR (*Looking all round*): The Boy . .! He's . . . gone!

34   EIGHT PLAYS FOR HAND PUPPETS

WIZARD: So he has, Bear! But never fear—I'll catch him on his way back through the wood. (WIZARD *and* BEAR *go out. Enter* DANNY).

DANNY: Thank goodness I'm past the wizard and the witch. Now I must find the owl and get the silver key for my box. (*Laughter from off stage*). Surely it can't be that silly boy again. (LAUGHING JACK *enters, laughing in the same infectious manner*). I'm off. I'm not wasting time on you! (*They both go off*).

SCENE 5.   Danny finds the owl.

(*An oak tree is placed against the back of the stage, so that* OWL *can put his head through top window and thus appears to be seated on oak branches*).

(DANNY *enters*).

DANNY: Ah! Here's a large oak tree. I'll call out and see if Mr. Owl lives in it. Oh, I had to knock three times. (*Knocks*). Mr. Owl! Mr. Owl!

OWL: Tu whit, tu whoo! Tu whit, tu whoo! What do you want, Boy?

DANNY: Please Mr. Owl, I want the silver key to unlock the box the postman brought me this morning. I believe you are the keeper of that key, Mr. Owl. May I have it, please?

OWL: Well, Boy, I'll fetch the key, but you'll have to answer three questions correctly before I hand it to you.

DANNY: I'll try, Mr. Owl. Ask me the first question.

OWL: What kind of a robbery is never dangerous?

DANNY: What kind of a robbery is never dangerous? Um-m. Is it a safe robbery?

OWL: A safe robbery! Quite correct, Boy. Now the next question—Which would burn longer, the candle on the birthday cake of a boy or a girl?

THE SILVER KEY

DANNY: Which would burn longer, the candle on the birthday cake of a boy or a girl? (*Pauses*). Neither. They would both burn shorter!

OWL: Clever Boy! They would both burn shorter. Here's the last question, my boy. Which bus crossed the ocean?

DANNY: That's easy, Mr. Owl. Colum . . . bus.

OWL: Good for you, Boy. Now I'll fetch the key. (OWL *disappears and* DANNY *waits impatiently,* OWL *reappears with key on a long cord*). I'll let it drop, Boy. There! Have you got it?

DANNY: Yes, thank you very much. Good-bye, Mr. Owl, and thank you again.

SCENE 6. Danny returns home.

DANNY (*He enters saying*: At last I've got the key. Now I must hurry home to open my box. (WIZARD *rushes in through opposite door and a chase ensues—in and out of doors—round and round stage*).

DANNY: My word! He nearly caught me. That was a lucky escape. I must watch out for the Witch now. (WITCH *appears hurriedly and with piercing screams. She also chases* DANNY *in and out of doors, round and round stage*).

WITCH: I missed him again. But he'll be back and then I will catch him. (*She goes out chuckling*). (DANNY *enters*).

DANNY: Here I am, back home at last. Mother, Mother! Here I am with my silver key.

MOTHER (*Pokes her head through top window*): There you are, Danny. I am pleased to see you. I'll come down at once and bring the box. (MOTHER *enters with box*).

36　　EIGHT PLAYS FOR HAND PUPPETS

DANNY: Let's undo it with the key, Mother. (*Much fumbling with key*). Look! Oh look, Mummy, what's inside! A drum. (*Brings it out*).

MOTHER: And a whistle. (*Brings out whistle*).

DANNY: Here's a pepper pot. (*Lifts it out*).

MOTHER: A label! What does it say?
"Sprinkle the powder on those who will come
When you blow this whistle and bang the drum."
I'll blow the whistle, Danny, and you bang the drum. (*They do so*). (*Enter* BEAR *and* BADGER).

DANNY: Look, Mother—the Witch's Badger and the Wizard's Bear. I met them in the woods. Let's put them in the box. In you go, Badger! In you go, Bear! Now I'll sprinkle the powder on them. (*Does so, and* MOTHER *and* DANNY *peer into the box*).

MOTHER: Danny! Look! A Princess! (PRINCESS *steps out of box*).

DANNY AND MOTHER (*Bowing*): Your Royal Highness!

PRINCESS: How happy I am to be changed back again from that horrid badger to my real self. The Witch changed me into a badger many months ago.

DANNY: I'll sprinkle some more powder into the box. (*Does so and out comes a* PRINCE).

DANNY AND MOTHER (*Bowing*): Your Royal Highness!

PRINCE: How happy I am to be a Prince again. The Wizard changed me into a bear many months ago.

PRINCESS: I do wish we had our dog Toby back—do you remember, Prince, he was with us in the wood the day we were caught by the witch and the wizard? (LAUGHING JACK *is heard laughing off stage*).

DANNY: It's that stupid boy again. I met him in the wood. I'll put him in our box. (*He does so and sprinkles on powder*).

THE SILVER KEY

LAUGHING JACK: Let me out! Let me out! (*Out comes dog* TOBY, *barking and yapping joyously*).

PRINCESS: Good dog! (*Pats him*). Get down, Toby! Good dog! (*To* DANNY *and* MOTHER). You must both come to our palace and my father will reward you handsomely for your excellent work this day. (DANNY *and* MOTHER *bow*. PRINCE *and* PRINCESS *go out of door, followed by* TOBY, DANNY *and* MOTHER).

THE END

PEPI AND SOMBRERO

by JOYCE THOMSON

This is another original play, full of warmth and colour, in which the real hero is a lively straw sombrero. There are no changes of scenery.

Characters: Pepi, a Mexican boy.

Granpa Gonzales, a nodding old Mexican.

Gendarme, a cowardly policeman with a very long nose and a sniff.

Bandit, who wears a mask and whose eyes gleam with sequins.

Sombrero, a hat made from flexible strawplait (of about $\frac{1}{2}''$ width), large enough to cover a puppet's head and shoulders, and with brightly coloured tassels on top.

Properties: Fruit stall

Gun

Cash box, large, black, clearly labelled "CASH".

Scenery: One arched exit at the back, with a side screen (wing) at either side. A large cactus growing out of a green and red stone to one side front.

PEPI AND SOMBRERO

(Guitar music or rhythmic tapping on a table. In whirls SOM-BRERO on a stick. He dances across and around the stage, then flits up to the top of side screen when the music stops. PEPI rushes in, calling and looking for him. Sombrero . . . Sombrero. . . . SOMBRERO hides behind screen, then peeps out again and is caught).

PEPI: Ah, there you are! You're naughty, hiding away from me like that. Don't want you now. *(Sulky)* You can go home and help granpa with his stall. *(SOMBRERO slides a little way down the side screen).*

PEPI: Go on . . . *(SOMBRERO droops sadly over the edge of screen. PEPI hastily strokes SOMBRERO).*

PEPI: Aw, don't be sad. I didn't mean it, honest. *(He kisses SOMBRERO and it straightens up).* There, now you are happy. Come on, let's play bandits. *(At the word "bandit", SOMBRERO is galvanised into action. He curls around PEPI and pulls him into hiding behind the far side screen. SOMBRERO looks out, showing most of himself to the audience. A gun appears across the doorway. It turns slowly in the hands of the bandit as he cautiously enters, training the gun in all directions).*

BANDIT: Huh! Nobody here. *(PEPI peeps. BANDIT swings around too late to catch him. Then SOMBRERO flicks his tassels).*

BANDIT: Who's that? Aw, just an old sombrero. *(Going over and prodding it).* The wind must have blown it. Looks like Pepi's. *(Turning from it)* I have business with his granpa today. *(Sinisterly)* *(There is a loud sniffing sound. BANDIT hides behind the cactus, gun trained towards the sound, as a long nose appears, followed by the rest of the* GENDARME. *He is so busy looking for clues up in the air, over the front of the stage and round the* SOMBRERO *he doesn't see* BANDIT, *who pokes his gun out further as* GENDARME *appears*).

BANDIT: Looking for someone?

GENDARME: Mmm. (*Looking on audience side of cactus*). A wicked bandit.

BANDIT: Me? (GENDARME *looks up and gasps with fright at the gun pointing at him*).

GENDARME: Y—y—y—yes (*The gun prods him*). Er—n—n—no—.

BANDIT: That's better.

GENDARME: P—p—p—please, don't point th—th—that gun at m—m—me.

BANDIT: I must, to shoot you.

GENDARME (*Falling at his feet*): Oh, please don't shoot me. Oh, think of my wife and children.

BANDIT: Bah! who cares about them?

GENDARME: P—p—p—please. I'll do anything you say.

BANDIT: Well . . .

GENDARME: P—p—please!

BANDIT: Maybe . . . *maybe*, I said, *if* you keep off this pitch this afternoon.

GENDARME: B—b—but this is Granpa Gonzales' pitch.

BANDIT: Si! I have business with Granpa Gonzales.

GENDARME: B—b—but he's an old man and . . .

BANDIT: And what? (*Prodding* GENDARME *with gun*).

GENDARME: Oh, n—n—nothing.

BANDIT: Aw, I'd better bump you off.

GENDARME: No, n—n—no, I promise. I won't come near here.

PEPI AND SOMBRERO   41

BANDIT: Hah! I believe you. You'd be too scared. (*He goes to exit and turns*). But if you do . . . (*Exit* BANDIT.

GENDARME *bursts into loud wailing and runs across the front of the stage*). Wa . . . aa . . . I'll never be a sergeant. Wa . . . aa . . . aa. (PEPI *and* SOMBRERO *rush in, one on either side of him, to comfort him*).

PEPI: Don't cry. We'll help you.

GENDARME: I'll never be a sergeant now. (*Sniffing*).

PEPI: Si, si! You must capture the bandit.

GENDARME: He m—m—might shoot me . . .

PEPI: What about my granpa? He m—might shoot *him*.

GENDARME: O—o—oh (*Weeps again*).

PEPI: You've got a gun. Why don't you use it?

GENDARME: I'm afraid of guns. I hate b—b—b—bangs.

PEPI: Aw, never mind. Sombrero will catch him for you.

GENDARME (*Moving away from* SOMBRERO): S—s—Sombrero?

PEPI: Si, si . . . he's magic. He can do anything. Go on, touch him. He won't hurt you. (GENDARME *pokes* SOMBRERO *and hastily jumps back.* SOMBRERO *pokes him back*).

GENDARME: He m—m—moved . . .

PEPI: Of course. He can do *anything*. He'll catch the bandit for you.

GENDARME: But *I* want to catch him (*Wailing voice*) or I'll never be a sergeant.

PEPI (*Paternally*): *You* can come and arrest him.

GENDARME: B—b—but I can't. He'll have a gun.

PEPI: No, he won't. You ask Sombrero. (GENDARME *looks at* SOMBRERO *who makes movement showing agreement with* PEPI).

42   EIGHT PLAYS FOR HAND PUPPETS

GENDARME: Oh, well, in that case . . . er, will there be
any danger? (*Anxiously*).

PEPI (*Sigh*): No. You can stay out of sight while there's
trouble.

GENDARME (*Happily*): Oh, good! I'd better clean up a
cell for him. (*Exit* GENDARME).

PEPI: Quick, Sombrero mio! We must warn Granpa.
(*Exit* PEPI, *followed by* SOMBRERO *who returns to doorway to give cheeky toss of tassels at audience. Enter* GRANPA
*pushing fruit-stall which he places on far front stage. Then
he brings out cash box, as from behind stall*).

GRANPA: Business is good. I have sold much fruit.
Now, let me see . . . I have taken one . . . three . . .
(*Enter* SOMBRERO *and cuddles up to* GRANPA).

GRANPA: Ah, hello, Sombrero mio! (*Patting it*) And
where is Pepi? (*Enter* PEPI, *breathless.* SOMBRERO *bobs
excitedly against* GRANPA *as* PEPI *talks*).

PEPI: Oh, granpa, there was a bandit and the gendarme is afraid of guns and he won't be here this
afternoon and . . .

GRANPA: Now, now, children, one at a time. Go and
sit down, Sombrero mio. (SOMBRERO *obeys. Sits on
cash box*).

PEPI: You mustn't stay here, granpa. The bandit's
going to rob you this afternoon.

GRANPA: Now, now, Pepi, you're imagining things
again.

PEPI: No, granpa, it's true. Ask Sombrero.

GRANPA: Is it true, Sombrero? (SOMBRERO *nods agreement*).

GRANPA: Oh dear . . . is he a nice bandit?

PEPI: Aw, granpa, of course not. He's a great big
wicked bandit.

PEPI AND SOMBRERO

43

GRANPA: Perhaps he just robs the rich to give to the poor.

PEPI: Huh! not this one! You ask Sombrero.

GRANPA: Is this true, Sombrero mio? (SOMBRERO *nods agreement*).

PEPI: There! I told you so. We must be quick. Have you got a gun, granpa?

GRANPA: Pepi! (*Shocked*).

PEPI: Well, the bandit *has*!

GRANPA: I am not afraid. Fetch me a good strong stick, Pepi.

PEPI: But I must stay and help you, Granpa . . . (SOMBRERO *is pushing* PEPI *towards exit*).

GRANPA: Look! Sombrero wants you to go. He will look after me.

PEPI: Well . . . if *you* say so, Sombrero. (*Exit* PEPI *crestfallen*).

GRANPA: That's a good Sombrero. You look after the cash box. The oranges are good today. A few more customers and they will all be sold. (GRANPA *nods thoughtfully over the oranges as* BANDIT *appears in doorway*).

BANDIT: Hey, you! Old man!

GRANPA: Ah, buenos dias, senor. You like to buy some oranges?

BANDIT: Hah! That's good, that is.

GRANPA: Si, the fruit is good, senor.

BANDIT: That's not what I meant. I want your *cash*.

GRANPA (*In a puzzled voice*): But that is not for sale, senor.

BANDIT: None of your funny stuff, old man. Get your hands up. (GRANPA *puts up his hands.* SOMBRERO *moves protectingly in front of him*).

BANDIT: And put down that sombrero.

44   EIGHT PLAYS FOR HAND PUPPETS

GRANPA: I am not touching it, senor.

BANDIT: Don't give me that! Get it out of the way or you'll both be full of holes.

GRANPA: Go, Sombrero mio! (SOMBRERO *dodges teasingly around the* BANDIT, *then flies to top of side screen*).

BANDIT: Huh! What's the trick, old man, how do you do it, eh?

GRANPA: There is no trick, senor. It moves by itself, senor.

BANDIT: Don't joke with me, old man. Stand over there! (GRANPA *moves to far side near the stall.* GENDARME *peeps in and dodges out hastily.* PEPI *peeps, while the* BANDIT *retreats towards the cactus, stopping at end of cash box nearest cactus. Meanwhile* SOMBRERO *has jumped down whizzing behind cactus and dropping down behind rock.* SOMBRERO *now taps the* BANDIT *in the back as he bends to pick up cash box. The* BANDIT *whirls around.* SOMBRERO *snatches away gun and pokes him in the stomach. The* BANDIT *doubles over with a groan. As he straightens up again,* SOMBRERO *whacks him over the head. The* BANDIT *totters, then falls over the front of the stage, and* SOMBRERO *sits on him. As* GRANPA *pulls cash box towards far side and sits on it,* PEPI *is persuading* GENDARME *to enter*).

PEPI (*To* GENDARME): Go on! Look! He can't hurt you now. Sombrero has his gun.

GENDARME: Oh, are you s—s—sure? (PEPI *pushing him in*).

PEPI: Of course. Take the gun and arrest him. (SOMBRERO *moves off the* BANDIT *and shoves the gun into* GENDARME's *hands which are still shaking*).

GENDARME: Don't push, Pepi. I'm not afraid. (*He goes over and prods the knocked out* BANDIT *with the gun*). Come on, I've a nice clean cell waiting for you.

PEPI AND SOMBRERO

BANDIT (*Contemptuously*): *You'd* never have got me if it wasn't for that . . . that . . . Sombrero. (GENDARME *prods him out*).

PEPI (*Rushes excitedly to* SOMBRERO *and hugs him*). Oh, Sombrero mio (*Kiss*) you were wonderful! Oh, Granpa, he's the best Sombrero in the whole world, isn't he?

GRANPA: Si. si. You are *both* good children. I don't know what I'd do without you. (*Both rush to hug him*). Now, now, children, what about helping me with the stall?

PEPI: Oh, we will, granpa. (*Music starts*).

PEPI: Listen! the fiesta has begun. Can we go, Granpa?

GRANPA: Si, si, my children. Sombrero, you take the cash box home for me. (SOMBRERO *turns upside down,* GRANPA *puts the cash box into him.* SOMBRERO *exits.* PEPI *takes out the stall, swaying in time with the music.* GRANPA *follows, nodding head to the rhythm.* SOMBRERO *returns to toss his tassels and make final exit.*

THE END

A CANADIAN FAIRY TALE

adapted by EDNA RIST

This simple play, with its flavour of an *Uncle Remus* story, has been adapted from a traditional Canadian story.

Characters: Jimmy Ginger (Property Boy)
Mrs. Goody
Mr. Rabbit
Mr. Fox
A Scarecrow

Properties: Carrots
A Lettuce or two
Small Christmas
  Trees
} these should fit securely into slots in the play-board
Watering can (with water)
Pot of Glue
Glue-brush
Sack.

Scene: Mrs. Goody's house, represented by the back-screen of the stage, with optional roof, door, window, etc. The action takes place in the garden in front of the house.

A CANADIAN FAIRY TALE

SCENE.   Mrs. Goody's garden.

(JIMMY GINGER *is planting some lettuce and carrots and a Christmas Tree in the garden. When he has finished he calls*):

JIMMY: Come on, Mrs. Goody. We're ready. Hurry up! The children are waiting.

MRS. GOODY: Don't hurry me so, Jimmy. You know I'm a poor old lady and can't hurry. (*Exit* JIMMY. MRS. GOODY *opens the window*).

MRS. GOODY: Ah! There you are children. How nice it is to see you. Can you see my nice lettuce and carrots? I should get a good price at the market for them. I think a little drop of water would do them good. Now, where is my watering can? Ah! Here it is. (*She comes out of her house with the watering can, waters the plants and puts the can down*).

MRS. GOODY: Do you know, children, there is a thief in my garden. He steals my lettuce and carrots. If you see him, just let me know. (*She goes indoors.* MR. RABBIT *pops up and steals lettuce. He nibbles at it*).

MR. RABBIT: Oh goody, goody! This *is* good. I'll take it home to all the other bunnies. (*Pops down*). (MRS. GOODY *peeps out of her window.*)

MRS. GOODY: I thought I heard something just then. Oh! my lettuce is gone, and you never told me, children! That's too bad. You might have told me! You tell me next time, please. (*She goes back from the window.* MR. RABBIT *pops up again. This goes on for some time until* MRS. GOODY *gets cross*).

MRS. GOODY: I know what to do! I'll get the scarecrow I've been making and put it in my garden. (*Fetches scarecrow*). Here it is. (*She fixes it in garden*).

48 EIGHT PLAYS FOR HAND PUPPETS

MRS. GOODY (*She laughs*): Someone is going to get a
surprise. You stay there, my pretty, and look after
my garden. Oh, but I haven't finished yet. Wait a
minute. (*She goes in and comes out with glue-pot and
brush. She stirs it well and begins to brush glue on to the*
SCARECROW). A little on his back. Now some on his
tummy. Ha, ha, ha. We'll see what we will see. (*She
goes indoors with pot and brush. Up pops* MR. RABBIT.
He looks at the Christmas Tree).

MR. RABBIT: What a nice Christmas tree Mrs. Goody
has here. (*He sees* SCARECROW *and is very frightened*).
Oh! whatever is it? Won't you tell me what it is?
Perhaps if I ask him very nicely he will get out of my
way. Get out of my way, please. Perhaps he is deaf in
that ear. I'd better try the other side. (*He goes to the
other side*). Hey! Mr. Scarecrow! Get out of my way!
(*Loud voice*). Oh! You won't, won't you? Take that
and that. (*He hits the* SCARECROW). (*He gets stuck on
the* SCARECROW). Let me go. Let me go! Mrs. Goody,
Friend Fox, come and help me. (MRS. GOODY *looks
out of her window*).

MRS. GOODY: I'm coming. I'm coming. (*She comes out
with a sack in her arms*).

MRS. GOODY: I've caught you, you little thief. (*She
puts the sack over the* RABBIT's *head. Then she pulls him off
the* SCARECROW. *She puts him on the playboard and
leaves him*).

MR. RABBIT: Friend Fox, Friend Fox, come and help
me. I don't like it in this sack. The fluff is getting all
up my nose. (*He sneezes. Enter* MR. FOX *singing. He
falls over the sack*).

MR. FOX: Hello! What have we here? Who is it? Does
anybody know?

MR. RABBIT: It's Mr. Rabbit. I'm in the sack.

A CANADIAN FAIRY TALE

Mr. Fox: Ah! I know you, Mr. Rabbit. What are you doing in that sack?

Mr. Rabbit: Well, you see, the old lady wants me to marry her daughter, and I don't want to.

Mr. Fox: I want a wife. I'll change places with you.

Mr. Rabbit: Will you? Will you really?

Mr. Fox: Yes, I will.

Mr. Rabbit: Come on, then. Be quick! Take hold of the corner of the sack and pull.

Mr. Fox: All right. (*He takes hold of the corner of the sack and pulls*).

Mr. Rabbit: I'm out. Now you get in. (*They change places*).

Mr. Fox: All right. I'm in.

Mr. Rabbit: Ha, ha. Your tail is sticking out.

Mr. Fox: Stick it in then. (Mr Rabbit *tries to stick the tail in the sack*).

Mr. Rabbit: I can't get it in. (*He swings up and down on the tail*).

Mr. Rabbit: See saw. See saw.

Mr. Fox: Stop it. You're hurting me.

Mr. Rabbit: Oh, I'm so sorry. I didn't mean to hurt you. I'd better be going. Goodbye. (*He goes off laughing to himself*).

Mr. Fox: Silly old thing. What is he laughing for, I wonder? It is hot in here. I wish the old lady would come. (Mrs. Goody *comes out with her saw*).

Mrs. Goody: I'm coming. I'm coming with my little saw. (*She starts to saw on the playboard*).

Mrs. Goody: What a lovely sound it makes!

Mr. Fox: What are you doing, old lady?

Mrs. Goody: Oh, I'm just sharpening my saw. What a lovely sound it makes, to be sure.

Mr. Fox: Why are you sharpening it?

50   EIGHT PLAYS FOR HAND PUPPETS

Mrs. Goody: I'm going to have rabbit pie for my supper tonight.

Mr. Fox: You are not, old lady.

Mrs. Goody: Oh yes, I am.

Mr. Fox: No, you are not.

Mrs. Goody: But I am. I put a rabbit in that sack.

Mr. Fox: We changed places. I'm a fox. Just look at my tail. (Mrs. Goody *looks at the* Fox's *tail*).

Mrs. Goody: Oh, yes. You are right. That is not a rabbit's tail. It is a fox's tail. Poor old thing. He must be suffocated in that sack. Let me pull it off. (*She pulls off the sack*). (*The* Fox *runs off without even a thank you*).

Mrs. Goody: What a silly old lady I am! I've lost the rabbit and the fox. Dear, dear. This is too much for me. I shall have to go in. Goodnight, everybody. Goodnight. (Mrs Goody *goes in, closes the window and draws to the curtains*).

THE END

THE GINGERBREAD BOY

A play by a Primary School child, showing what can be done with the simplest of well-known rhymes. This retains the pace and the repetitive rhyming of the original, and gives scope for an exciting chase in and out of the stage. It is interesting in its use of the Narrator, who, being more or less outside the play, is in a good position to point out that the Fox's lies are not acceptable to our own code of behaviour.

Characters: Narrator
Old Woman
Old Man
Voice
Gingerbread Boy
Cow
Horse
Fox
Little Boy.

Properties: Cupboard
Telephone
Broom
Purse, or Money
Currants
Carrot
Knife.

Scenes: 1. The Old Woman's house.
2. Outside.

SCENE 1

NARRATOR: Once upon a time there lived an old woman and an old man. They were often very sad because they had no baby. One day the little old woman thought she would make a gingerbread boy. Ah, here comes the little old woman now. (*The little* OLD WOMAN *comes in shivering*).

OLD WOMAN: It is cold to-day. Now what shall I make for my husband's tea? Ah, I'll make some gingerbread. (*The* OLD WOMAN *goes to the food cupboard*). Oh, I haven't any ginger left. I will 'phone up to the baker's shop. (*The* OLD WOMAN *goes to the 'phone*). Yes, Popcorn 146 please. (*There is a pause*). Is that you, Mr. Popcorn? Could you send someone round to my house with some ginger? (*There is a pause*). Yes, thank you. (*The* OLD WOMAN *starts to sweep the floor and hums a little tune*). Ah, I shall make a gingerbread boy. When the boy comes with the ginger, I shall start on him. (*There is a knocking on the door*). There is the boy. Now I shall start on the gingerbread boy. He shall be my very own boy. (*The* OLD WOMAN *goes to the door*). Thank you. How much money will that be? (*There is a voice heard at the door*).

VOICE: Two shillings and sixpence, please.

OLD WOMAN: There you are. (*There is a pause and the* OLD WOMAN *goes back to her kitchen*). Now I shall start on my little gingerbread boy. (*She starts to hum a little tune again*). Now, what shall I use for his eyes?

NARRATOR: Have two currants, old woman.

THE GINGERBREAD BOY   53

OLD WOMAN: Yes, that will be a good idea. There, now I will have a carrot for his nose. Now, what shall I have for a mouth?

NARRATOR: I should put a slit, old woman.

OLD WOMAN: Yes, I will do that, thank you. Now I shall put him in the oven.

SCENE 2

NARRATOR: Old Woman, I think your little boy is done. (*The* OLD WOMAN *goes to the oven*).

OLD WOMAN: No, it is not done yet, but it is nearly done. (*She sits down in a chair*).

NARRATOR: Oh, I think your little boy is burning. (*The* OLD WOMAN *goes to the oven again*).

OLD WOMAN: Yes, you are right this time, it is done. (*She goes to the oven, takes out the gingerbread. But the little gingerbread boy skips round the room*).

GINGERBREAD BOY: Hello, little old woman, what are you frightened about?

OLD WOMAN: N—n—nothing, s—s—son.

GINGERBREAD BOY: I'm not your son. Goodbye, I'm going out.

OLD WOMAN: Where are you going to?

GINGERBREAD BOY: I am going away, little old woman.

OLD WOMAN: Come back, come back.

GINGERBREAD BOY: Run, run as fast as you can, you can't catch me, I'm the gingerbread man. (*The* OLD WOMAN *starts to cry. Then the husband comes in*).

OLD MAN: What is the matter, my dear?

OLD WOMAN: I—I—I b—baked a g—g—ginger—b—b—bread boy a—and w—when I o—o—opened the o—o—oven door h—h—he s—skipped o—out.

54 EIGHT PLAYS FOR HAND PUPPETS

OLD MAN: Where did he go?

OLD WOMAN: I—I d—don't know, h—he w—went out of the d—door.

OLD MAN: Well, let us run after him, dear.

OLD WOMAN: Yes, he ran round the corner. (*They both run out calling*—).

OLD MAN ⎫
OLD WOMAN ⎭ Stop, stop!

GINGERBREAD BOY: Run, run as fast as you can, you can't catch me, I'm the gingerbread man. (*Suddenly the little gingerbread boy stops*).
Ah, here's a bench I can sit on till I get my breath back. What's that noise? It's a c—c—cow.

COW: Moo—moo—moo. Ah, here is a little gingerbread man. Stop, stop, little gingerbread man, I want to eat you for my lunch. Moo—moo—moo.

GINGERBREAD BOY: Run, run as fast as you can, you can't catch me, I'm the gingerbread man.

COW: Stop, stop!

OLD WOMAN: Stop, stop!

GINGERBREAD BOY: Run, run as fast as you can, you can't catch me, I'm the gingerbread man. (*The little* GINGERBREAD BOY *stops again*). Oh, I'm out of breath again. What's that noise? It's a horse.

HORSE: Hee—haw, hee—haw. Stop, little gingerbread boy, I want to eat you.

GINGERBREAD BOY: Run, run as fast as you can, you can't catch me, I'm the gingerbread man.

HORSE: Stop, stop!

COW: Stop, stop!

OLD MAN: Stop, stop!

OLD WOMAN: Stop, stop!

THE GINGERBREAD BOY

55

GINGERBREAD BOY: Run, run as fast as you can, you can't catch me, I'm the gingerbread man (*He stops*). Oh, what's this, a little boy playing with his soldiers, now what am I going to do? (*The* LITTLE BOY *looks up and sees the* GINGERBREAD BOY).

BOY: Oh, stop, little gingerbread boy, I want to eat you.

GINGERBREAD BOY: Run, run as fast as you can, you can't catch me, I'm the gingerbread man.

BOY: Stop, stop!

HORSE: Stop, stop!

COW: Stop, stop!

OLD MAN: Stop, stop!

OLD WOMAN: Stop, stop!

GINGERBREAD BOY: Run, run as fast as you can, you can't catch me, I'm the gingerbread man. (*He stops*). Oh, I am out of breath again and I can't go any farther because of that river. (*A* FOX *appears and the little* GINGERBREAD BOY *looks frightened*).

GINGERBREAD BOY: Oh, please Mr. Fox, don't eat me. If you leave me until I am fatter then you may— — —

FOX: I don't want to eat you, little gingerbread boy.

GINGEBREAD BOY: Not even when I am fatter?

FOX: No.

GINGERBREAD BOY: Oh, you are kind Mr. Fox, but it does not help because I shall soon be eaten up by the others. I can't go any farther because of the river.

FOX: Who are the others?

GINGERBREAD BOY: The old woman, the old man, the cow, the horse and the little boy.

FOX: I shall take you across the river, little gingerbread boy.

GINGERBREAD BOY: Oh, thank you, Mr. Fox.

56 EIGHT PLAYS FOR HAND PUPPETS

Fox: Oh, don't thank me; it's quite all right. Jump on to my tail. (*They go a little farther*). Oh, my tail is going under the water, jump on to my back. (*Pause*). Oh, my back is going under water, jump on to my head. (*Pause*). Oh, my head is going under the water, jump on my tongue. (*All of a sudden the* Fox *snaps his jaws*). Snap.

Gingerbread Boy: Oh, I am a quarter gone.

Fox: Snap!

Gingerbread Boy: Oh, I am a half gone.

Fox: Snap!

Gingerbread Boy: Oh, I am three-quarters gone.

Fox: Snap!

Gingerbread Boy: Oh, I am all gone. (The Horse *comes in*).

Horse: Have you seen the gingerbread boy, Mr. Fox?

Fox: No, I haven't seen him. He may have drowned, there's a river over there. (*The* Cow *comes in*).

Cow: Moo—moo, have you seen the gingerbread boy?

Fox: No. He may have drowned. There's a river over there.

Boy: Have you seen the gingerbread boy, Mr. Fox?

Fox: No. He may have drowned. There's a river over there.

Old Man: Have you seen my wife's gingerbread boy?

Fox: No. He may have drowned. There's a river over there.

Old Woman: Have you seen the gingerbread boy?

Fox: No, he may have drowned. There's a river over there. (*The* Old Woman *goes out crying*).

Narrator: You wicked old fox, you know where the gingerbread boy is.

Fox: Yes, he tasted lovely.

THE END

THE EGG

by Violet M. Philpott

This is an entirely original play using only animal characters. It can be produced by a solo puppeteer or by a group.

Characters: Polly Parrot
Monkey
Lion
Bandicoot: a baby creature, a little like a blue-grey mouse, with long floppy ears (found in India and Australia).
Baby Parrot
Tropical Flies.

Properties: Nest
Parrot's Egg
Eggshell (half)
Coconut
Grass
Balloon: orange colour.

Scenery: Sandbank with dark hole in it
Palm Tree: this should fit into slot on one side of stage, so that it can be lifted out by puppet and carried off.

58　　EIGHT PLAYS FOR HAND PUPPETS

Scene opens showing POLLY'S *nest on one side* (*front*) *and a palm tree on the other. Attached to the back-screen is a sandbank with a dark hole in it.*

(*One or more large, colorful,* TROPICAL FLIES *appear and buzz about, settling here and there, then flying off again*).

POLLY: (*Singing off-stage*): Today I feel so happy, so happy, so happy . . . (*Entering*). Today I feel so happy . . . (FLIES *settle and annoy her as she sits on nest*). Oh, go away flies! (FLIES *continue to annoy until she chases them. Exit* FLIES). (*A deep* "Hi Ho Hum" *is heard distantly off stage, coming nearer*).

POLLY: That sounds like Lion coming.

LION (*Entering*): Hello, Polly.

POLLY: Hello, Lion.

LION: Polly! Could you . . . would you . . . let me see your egg?

POLLY: My egg? Who told you I'd laid an egg?

LION: Oh, everyone in the jungle knows you've laid an egg.

POLLY: Oh, *do* they!

LION: Yes, Polly. Let me have a look.

POLLY: Well, just a *little* look, Lion. (*She moves aside just long enough for* LION *to have a quick peep at egg*).

LION: Well! it was a lovely egg, Polly, what I could see of it!

POLLY: Thank you, Lion.

LION: And Polly . . .

POLLY: Yes, Lion?

LION: Do you think I could have the palm tree over there by the rock?

POLLY: The Palm tree? What ever for, Lion?

THE EGG   59

LION: Well, I'm building myself a nice new den, and it would be very useful for holding the roof up.

POLLY: Oh, all right, Lion, you can have the tree.

LION: Thank you, Polly. I'll be back for that presently. Goodbye!

POLLY: Goodbye, Lion! (*Exit* LION). I think I'll just go and see if I can find a nice fresh cucumber to make some sandwiches for tea. (*Exit* POLLY). (BANDICOOT *peeps round edge of Exit, then cautiously approaches centre stage and surveys audience, turns and sees nest and sniffs his way towards it*).

BANDICOOT: Oh! It's a nest. I'm going to put some grass in it. (*Exits, returns with some grass*). There's *some* grass. I'm going to get some *more* grass now. (*Exits*, returns with larger quantity of grass). Look! its got flowers in it. (*Puts grass on nest*). Now I'll get *one more* lot of grass. (*Exits, returning with large quantity of grass held on top of head*). I feel tired now. I think I'll go to sleep. I'll cover my eyes with my ears—it keeps the light out. (*Lies on nest. Slow breathing movements show he is almost asleep*). *Enter* POLLY, *carrying large cucumber*).

POLLY: What are you doing in my nest?

BANDICOOT (*Scared*): I didn't know it was *your* nest, Polly.

POLLY: You might have broken my egg.

BANDICOOT: I didn't know you had an egg in it.

POLLY: You should use those big eyes of yours. Now just take all this mess out of here.

BANDICOOT: But I only just put it in.

POLLY: Then you can only just take it out again. Come on! (*Begins to remove grass and hand it to him*).

BANDICOOT: Oh, all right, Polly. I'm sorry. (*Goes off with grass*). (POLLY *goes off, returning with a brush to*

egg, it's gone! It's that naughty Bandicoot. (*Calls at door*): Lion! Lion! Come quickly! (*Enter* LION).

LION: What ever is the matter, Polly? We can hear you all over the jungle!

POLLY: It's that naughty Bandicoot. He's taken my egg.

LION: Oh, no, he hasn't. He's been with me, helping me build my den.

POLLY: Well, *somebody's* taken it. (*To audience*:) Did *you* take it?

AUDIENCE: No! The Monkey took it! etcetera.

LION: *Who* took it?

AUDIENCE: The Monkey.

POLLY: Oh, my lovely egg!

LION: Never mind, Polly. I'll help you to look for it. I expect Monkey has hidden it. You know what Monkey is like! Let's look in the hole in the old rock. (*Looks*). No! It's not *there*.

POLLY: Oh, *do* something, Lion, *do* something.

LION (*After thinking for a moment*): I know, Polly. (*To audience*): If you see Monkey, will you all call Polly?

AUDIENCE: Yes!

LION: Come on, Polly. I'll help you look for it, and if anyone sees Monkey they will call you. (LION *and* POLLY *exit*). (*Enter* MONKEY *carrying egg. The audience calls* "Polly!" POLLY *enters but* MONKEY *has already gone again. This can be repeated several times, developing into a chase.* MONKEY *sometimes behind* POLLY *and disappearing when audience calls* "Behind you!").

POLLY: (*Going off, tells audience to call her more quickly*).

(*Enter* MONKEY *and puts egg in hole in rock.* POLLY *returns as audience calls but fails to catch* MONKEY). (*At this point there is usually spontaneous help from audience, or* POLLY *can ask* "Where is it?").

THE EGG   63

AUDIENCE: In the rock (etc.) . . .

POLLY: Oh, my lovely egg. (*Tries to rescue it*). I can't reach it! (*Calls*). Lion! Lion! (*Enter* LION).

LION: Have you found it, Polly?

POLLY: Yes. It's in the rock.

LION: No, it isn't. I looked *there*!

POLLY: It *is*.

LION (*Looking in hole*): So it is. Well! you silly bird. Take it out.

POLLY: I can't, Lion. I can't reach it.

LION: Well, never mind. I'll get it for you. (LION *puts paw into hole and becomes stuck*). Oh, help, help! I'm stuck! (POLLY *pulls him by his tail and eventually frees him*). Oh, my poor paw, my poor tail!

POLLY: What about my poor *egg*!

LION: Oh, yes, your egg.

POLLY: *Do* something, Lion, *do* something!

LION (*After a little thought*): I know, Polly! I'm so strong, I'll just knock the rock down!

POLLY: No! You're so strong you'd *break* my egg!

LION: Oh dear! I hadn't thought of that.

POLLY (*Weeping*): My poor egg, my poor egg! (*She sits with back to audience*. LION *puts arm round her comfortingly*).

LION (*Suddenly*): I know! *Bandicoot*!

POLLY: Bandicoot? But he's only a baby!

LION: I don't care. He's very helpful. He's been helping me build my den.

POLLY: Well! Get him, Lion. Hurry up! (*Exit* LION).

LION: All right, Polly. (POLLY *looks into hole again*).

POLLY: Oh! I do wish that Bandicoot would hurry up and come. (*Enter* BANDICOOT *out of breath*).

BANDICOOT: Hello, Polly, Lion says you want me . . . and I ran all the way!

64   EIGHT PLAYS FOR HAND PUPPETS

POLLY: Oh, you are a good little thing. Look in here. (*Points in hole*)

BANDICOOT (*Looking in hole*): It's an *egg*!

POLLY: Of course it's an egg. It's *my* egg! *Monkey* put it in and I want *you* to take it out.

BANDICOOT: I'll try, Polly, I'll try.

POLLY: Oh, I can't bear to look! (*Goes off-stage. For solo performer this is in order to have spare hand to help push egg into* BANDICOOT's *paws from soft 'pocket' in hole*).

BANDICOOT: I've got it, Polly! I've got it!

POLLY (*As she re-enters*). Careful! Careful!

BANDICOOT (*Carrying egg carefully to nest*): There you are, Polly.

POLLY: Oh, you are a good little thing. (*Kisses him*).

BANDICOOT: Well, I must go to help Lion finish his den now. Bye-bye! (*Exit*).

POLLY: Bye-bye, Bandi. (*She sits on nest*). And I'll never, never, leave my egg again. (*A sound of cracking is heard*). What's that? (*Looks in nest*). It's my egg! It's breaking! Ah! Come to mummy then! (*Baby Polly appears from nest, with half of eggshell over its head*). There! take the eggshell off your head! (*Picks it up after removing shell, just as* BANDICOOT *re-enters*).

BANDICOOT: Oh, Polly! You've got a *baby* Polly!

POLLY: Yes, Bandi, thanks to you. You were just in time.

BANDICOOT: Lion has finished his den now and says will you come to tea. And bring baby Polly!

POLLY: Of course, Bandi. You lead the way.

BANDICOOT: Won't Lion be surprised! (*To audience*) Bye-bye! Bye-bye! (*Exeunt*).

THE END

THE LONELY GIANT

by the E.P.A. London Group

This play is based on an original theme by Violet Philpott, one of the members of the Group. It is particularly interesting for its introduction of a human actor into the puppet stage, as the Giant.

As a prelude to the original performance, the Giant sang his song off-stage. (Guitar, etc., accompaniment optional). The words can easily be adapted to a traditional tune such as the *Jolly Miller*, but any group lucky enough to have its own composer can have the words set to an original tune.

If the play is performed by children used to part-singing, then the song can be adapted for several voices; alternatively some pastoral music could be played on bamboo pipes or recorders in place of the song.

There is no change of scenery.

Characters: The Lonely Giant (played by a human)
               Molly, a village girl
               Jenny, her friend
               A variety of small animals (rabbit with baby rabbits, a squirrel, a tortoise, perhaps a hen and chickens)
               Mouse
               Bear
               Wolf

EIGHT PLAYS FOR HAND PUPPETS

Properties: Basket of flowers
Food for animals: biscuit crumbs, cheese, celery, lettuce, nuts, sweets, etc.
Soap flakes—large packet labelled ONO
Soap flakes—large packet labelled OHO
Jersey—puppet size replica of that worn by the Giant
String of gold beads, large and heavy
A small replica string of gold beads.

Scenery: To one side of the stage, front corner, a willow tree and some bulrushes to indicate a pond.
At the other side and to the rear, a large cave with curtained entrance.

SONG

'THE LONELY GIANT'

There was a lonely giant once, a kindly one was he,
His home a cave beside a lake—no human friends
    had he.
His only friends were creatures small
That he could hardly see;
The mouse, the mole, the bear, the fox,
The hen and her chickens three.
    (Repeat tune for last four lines)
But other friends he longed to have to keep him
    company,
And how his dreams at last came true, you are
    about to see.

Note: additional characters may be added to cast, as mentioned in song.

THE LONELY GIANT

Enter MOLLY (*Calling to her friend*): Come along, Jenny. This is the place I told you about.

Enter JENNY (*Carrying basket*): But you are quite sure it's true about the pond?

MOLLY: Yes. My mother says that if you look in the pond on this day of the year you will see the face of the man you are going to marry.

JENNY: I don't believe it!

MOLLY: You're afraid to look!

JENNY: Well, you look first.

MOLLY: Oh, all right. (*She peers down into pond*).

JENNY: Do you see anything?

MOLLY: No, I don't see anybody.

JENNY: Te—he—he! You aren't going to get married at all!

MOLLY: Well, now it's your turn!

JENNY: Oh no, I'm not going to look. It's just silly!

MOLLY: Well, come along then, we had better be going back to the village.

JENNY: I want to stay for a while. I'll just sit here for a bit. (*Puts down her basket of flowers*).

MOLLY: Oh, all right. But you had better be careful. They say there's a giant lives near here.

JENNY: A giant? I don't believe that either. I'm not afraid of giants.

MOLLY: Well, if you are sure you are not coming, I'm off. Goodbye.

68 EIGHT PLAYS FOR HAND PUPPETS

JENNY: Goodbye, Molly. (*Exit* MOLLY). (*Brief pause*).
Now she's gone I will take a peep. (*She bends over the
water, and, as she does so, the* GIANT *appears from his cave
and leans over her, also looking in the water. She sees his
reflection and screams*).

GIANT: Don't be afraid. I won't hurt you. I know all
the village people are afraid of me and think that
because I'm so big I shall hurt them. But I *like*
people and only want to be friends with them. That
is why I'm so lonely. Won't you stay and talk to me?

JENNY: Oh, no, I must be going.

GIANT (*Picks up her basket and holds it high above her,
teasingly*). Now you can't go.

JENNY: Oh, please give me back my basket.

GIANT: Only if you promise to stay a little while and
talk to me. I get so lonely and have only the animals
for company. My goodness! I nearly forgot! It is
their feeding time. Would you like to stay and
watch?

JENNY: Do you feed the animals? How lovely!

GIANT: Yes. And Mouse is first. Here he comes now.
(MOUSE *appears from a hole in* GIANT'S *jersey. He holds
it tenderly and strokes it*).

JENNY: Oh, help! A mouse!

GIANT: What! Are you afraid of a tiny mouse too? *He*
can't hurt you. Come and stroke him.

JENNY: Oh no, I couldn't.

GIANT (*Feeds the* MOUSE *with biscuit crumbs and cheese*):
There, that's all for now, Mouse. Off you go.
(MOUSE *returns to hole in jersey*). And now I must
fetch my musical box to call the others. Excuse me a
moment . . . (*Goes into cave and returns with musical box*).
Listen!

JENNY: What a pretty tune.

THE LONELY GIANT

GIANT: Ah! and here come some more of the animals. Mrs. Rabbit and her babies, early as usual, and very hungry no doubt. Here you are, my friends! (*He feeds them with pieces of lettuce, celery, etc.*) More? Very well, here you are . . . (*At last Mrs. Rabbit rounds up the babies and escorts them away*). Goodbye, see you tomorrow!

JENNY: Aren't they nice!

GIANT: Yes, and here comes Squirrel for some nuts. Hallo, Squirrel. Here you are, help yourself. (*Offers bag of nuts*). Had enough? Take some home with you. Goodbye, goodbye. (*Exit* SQUIRREL).

GIANT: Ah, here's Bear. Hallo, Bear, would you like some candy? I've run out of honey. Here you are. Let me take the paper off for you. (BEAR *eats with grunts of relish, departs with candy in paper bag*). Bye, Bear, be seeing you! I wonder who's next? (*Enter* WOLF *disguised by a sheepskin over head and back*).

GIANT (*As* WOLF *comes to the front*): Ah-ha, my friend who is not my friend, I believe. (*His large hand grasps the* WOLF *securely*). When you learn to behave better and not chase the other animals you can join the queue. But now, be off with you! (*Releases* WOLF).

WOLF (*Turning at exit*): I'll pay you back, you see if I don't!

GIANT (*Moving hand towards* WOLF): Go on, off with you. (*Exit* WOLF). (*To Girl*). I think that must be all for today.

JENNY: How kind of you to feed the animals. You really are a nice giant after all.

GIANT: And are you not afraid of me any more?

JENNY: No.

70   EIGHT PLAYS FOR HAND PUPPETS

GIANT: Then touch my hand, just to show we're friends.

JENNY: (*Shy and hesitant, slowly plucks up courage and touches* GIANT's *hand, which he carefully keeps quite still*).

GIANT: There, you see, it's *quite* safe! And now we are friends.

JENNY: You don't look after *yourself* very well. Look how dirty your jersey is, *and* full of holes.

GIANT: Holes? Oh, that's where Mouse comes in and out. He likes the warmth inside.

JENNY: If you like, I'll wash it for you.

GIANT: Would you really? But I'm afraid I haven't any soap left. You see, I can't go into the village for any because the people are all so afraid of me.

JENNY: Well, I'll get a packet of soap flakes for you, giant size. We shall need a very big bowl!

GIANT: We could wash it in the pond. There's plenty of water in it.

JENNY: All right. I will be as quick as I can. Goodbye!

GIANT: Goodbye, and thank you so much! (*Exit* JENNY). (GIANT *hums cheerfully to himself*). At last I have a human friend. What a nice girl she is. I forgot to ask her name. Perhaps she will stay to tea. I'll fill the kettle. (*Fetches large kettle, dips it in the pond and returns it to the cave*).

JENNY (*Returning*): Here it is, the largest packet I could get. (*The packet is labelled* "O H O"). (*Whistling of kettle is heard*).

GIANT: Tea time! Would you like to come in my cave and have tea with me? It's not very tidy, and I have only big cups . . .

JENNY: Oh, thank you. And then we must wash the jersey so that it can be drying.

THE LONELY GIANT

GIANT: Then come along in. (*They go inside the cave, leaving the packet of soap-flakes front centre*). (*Enter* WOLF, *after peering cautiously around*).

WOLF: Ha ha! I'll get even with you, Mr. Giant. (*He removes the packet of* "O H O" *and substitutes packet labelled* "O N O" *and exits with self-satisfied laugh*). (GIANT *and* JENNY *come out of cave*).

JENNY: That *was* a lovely cup of tea. And now we must get on with the washing. Will you put the soap flakes in the pond and stir it, and then take off your jersey. (GIANT—*business of opening packet, sprinkling, stirring with a stick—bucket of water held below-stage—and, optionally, bubbles rising.* GIANT *then goes into cave, removes jersey and hands it to* JENNY).

JENNY: Oh, isn't it heavy! *You* must put it in the pond.

GIANT (*Reappearing in shirt*): All right, leave it to me. It will be even heavier when it is wet. (*Drops jersey into pond, pokes and stirs*).

JENNY: While it is soaking I'll help you wash up the tea things.

GIANT: Oh, thank you. Do you know, I don't even know your name.

JENNY: I'm Jenny.

GIANT (*Tenderly*): Jenny! What a lovely name.

JENNY: And what is *your* name?

GIANT: I've forgotten! It is such a long time since anyone called me by my name. And as I am the last of the Giants I can't be mistaken for any one else.

JENNY: Well, I'm going to call you Gerald.

GIANT: That will be nice.

JENNY: Now let us do the washing up. Then we—or you—can take out the jersey. (JENNY *and* GIANT *enter cave. There is the clatter of crockery for a moment or two, then they reappear*).

72 EIGHT PLAYS FOR HAND PUPPETS

JENNY: Now we will see if the jersey is clean. (*Peers into pond*). That's funny! I can't see it.

GIANT (*Also looking in pond*): But it must be there! (*Puts his hand in water, feels around, then pulls out a very small—puppet size—jersey, and holds it up in astonishment*). My jersey, it has shrunk!

JENNY: Oh, I'm *so* sorry, Gerald. But I can't understand it. O H O is the best brand there is.

GIANT (*Picking up the empty box and reading the label*). This says O—N—O, O N O, not O H O.

JENNY: But I *know* I got O H O. Someone must have changed it while we were in the cave.

GIANT: You're right, and I have a good idea who it was!

JENNY: Well, you can't wear it now. I shall have to knit you another one.

GIANT: But that would take you years. And where will Mouse live now?

JENNY (*Starts to cry*). Oh, I'm *so* sorry!

GIANT: There, there, never mind. It *was* a very old jersey anyway. Cheer up and I'll give you a nice present. (*He pops in cave and emerges holding a long and heavy string of gold beads*). Here you are; it was my giant grandmother's. (*Hands it to* JENNY).

JENNY (*Reaching out for beads*): Oh, Isn't it lovely! But it is so heavy. Oh! (*She drops it and it falls into the pond*). Oh, dear, oh dear! (*Cries*).

GIANT: Don't cry, Jenny. I'll get it back for you. (*He dives in the pond with a large splash and disappears. There are gurgling sounds*).

JENNY (*Looking in pond*): Gerald, where are you? Oh, dear, I can't see him! (*A small hand appears over edge of pond, followed by another, and then by a small replica of*

THE LONELY GIANT

the giant's head, and instinctively JENNY *helps him out. In his hand is a small replica of the beads).*

GIANT: Why! How big you've become!

JENNY: Oh, no! It is you who have become small! And you are so wet!

GIANT: Oh, that doesn't matter. Here are your beads!

JENNY: Oh, Gerald! They are the right size now. It was the water! Everything shrinks in it.

GIANT: Well, now I shall be able to wear my jersey again. And . . . and . . .

JENNY: What is it, Gerald?

GIANT: It's wonderful! Now I am the same size as you, Jenny, and nobody will be frightened of me any more, and I can ask you to marry me! *Will* you marry me, Jenny?

JENNY: Oh, Gerald, of course I will. (*They embrace shyly*).

GIANT: I must tell all the animals! I'll get the musical box. (*Enters cave*). Oh, it's so large and heavy now. Come and help me. (JENNY *enters cave and they reappear carrying the box, lift its lid so that the music begins . . . and slowly the animals return. . . . As the animals gather they murmur among themselves, and at last the* BEAR *says*): Where is the Giant?

GIANT: Here I am.

BEAR: You aren't a Giant.

GIANT: But I *was* the Giant!

JENNY: Yes, that's right. He jumped in the pond, which must have had some magic powder in it, and came out small, just like the jersey and the beads!

BEAR (*Looking closely at* GIANT): Um! You're face *is* like Giant's . . .

74 EIGHT PLAYS FOR HAND PUPPETS

GIANT: I am—or I was—the Giant. But now I am going to marry Jenny, and I would like you all to come to our wedding.

ANIMALS (*In chorus*): Hooray for the Giant and Jenny! How nice!

WOLF (*From rear*): What about me? Can I come to the wedding, too? If it wasn't for me you would still be a Giant. I changed the powder!

GIANT: I guessed as much. Well, all's well that ends well. So let's all be friends. Now we will go to the village for the wedding.

(*The* BEAR *picks up the musical box, a procession is formed, the* GIANT *and* JENNY *lead out with the* BEAR *coming last*).

THE END